Communications in Computer and Information Science 1650

Evi Zouganeli · Anis Yazidi · Gustavo Mello ·
Pedro Lind (Eds.)

Nordic Artificial Intelligence Research and Development

4th Symposium of the Norwegian AI Society, NAIS 2022
Oslo, Norway, May 31 – June 1, 2022
Revised Selected Papers

 Springer

Editors
Evi Zouganeli
Department of Mechanical, Electronics,
and Chemical Engineering
Oslo Metropolitan University
Oslo, Norway

Gustavo Mello
Department of Computer Science
Oslo Metropolitan University
Oslo, Norway

Anis Yazidi
Department of Computer Science
Oslo Metropolitan University
Oslo, Norway

Pedro Lind
Department of Computer Science
Oslo Metropolitan University
Oslo, Norway

ISSN 1865-0929   ISSN 1865-0937 (electronic)
Communications in Computer and Information Science
ISBN 978-3-031-17029-4   ISBN 978-3-031-17030-0 (eBook)
https://doi.org/10.1007/978-3-031-17030-0

This Springer imprint is published by the registered company Springer Nature Switzerland AG
The registered company address is: Gewerbestrasse 11, 6330 Cham, Switzerland

Preface

This volume contains the papers presented during the 2022 Symposium of the Norwegian AI Society (NAIS 2022) that was held at Oslo Metropolitan University (OsloMet), in Oslo, during May 31 – June 1, 2022, and organized jointly by OsloMet and Simula Metropolitan (SimulaMet). The NAIS Symposium was held for the fourth time, and the second time since 2010. The previous symposium was held in Trondheim in 2019 as the COVID-19 pandemic forced us to cancel in 2020 and 2021. The symposium aims at bringing together researchers and practitioners in the field of artificial intelligence (AI) from Norway and Scandinavia to present ongoing work and discuss the future of AI. With the symposium, NAIS provides a forum for networking among researchers as well as building links with related research fields, practitioners, businesses, and the public sector.

This year there were 17 submissions. Each submission was reviewed by at least two Program Committee members as well as one of the symposium co-chairs. The quality of the submissions was very high, and 11 papers were finally accepted for publication, which were presented in four technical sessions – two on Tuesday, May 31, and two on Wednesday, June 1. The program included four invited keynote talks and a commercial pitch and panel session. In addition, three tutorials were offered before the start and after the end of the main event.

The symposium started at noon on Tuesday with a welcome address by symposium co-chair Evi Zouganeli. The first part of the symposium was dedicated to applied AI and robotics for real-life applications. The first keynote was given by Filippo Sanfilippo, University of Agder, who discussed different technologies, types of robots, and their applications including in Industry 5.0, wearable robotics, intelligent health, human-robot interaction and collaboration, and search-and-rescue scenarios. This keynote was the perfect introduction to the following pitch and panel discussion on "AI- and robotics-enabled systems – status, barriers, and timeline for deployment in real-life systems". The session was introduced by Evi Zouganeli and included three pitch presentations. Nils Jacob Berland, CEO, presented the autonomous power-line inspection solution by Bergen Robotics AS. He discussed the capabilities of the drone-based system, and the hurdles encountered on the way to development and real deployment. Audun Sanderud, CEO, presented the social robotics solution by Hiro Futures AS. He discussed the rationale and the technology behind robots that engage human like body language to facilitate communication and interaction. Asgeir Berland, Lead Data Scientist, presented the warehouse logistics and groceries distribution solution by Oda AS. He discussed how AI powers efficient resource management, route optimization, and distribution of fresh goods in Norway.

Thereafter, the three commercial representatives, together with Filippo Sanfilippo, had a panel discussion that was moderated by Trym Lindell, OsloMet. Amongst other things, the discussion revolved around the transformative power of AI for our society, and the potential for significant new value creation. What decides the timeline for deployment – is it management, market acceptance, or technical maturity? The panelists discussed having underestimated various technical challenges that may appear trivial but can delay or even hamper real deployments. Aspects that are trivial for humans are extremely challenging in artificial systems, where a reliable and safe operation is required in the vicinity of humans. Explainability, trustworthiness, safety, and regulation were mentioned as important stepstones. In addition, the discussion touched upon the effect of AI-uptake on the job market – our panelists seemed to agree that robots will be assigned the boring repetitive tasks and allow the humans to shine. Overall, the panel shed new and insightful light on important topics around the roadmap towards real-life deployment.

Two technical sessions followed, one on Robotics and Intelligent Systems that was chaired by Kai Olav Ellefsen, University of Oslo, and one on AI in Cyber and Digital Sphere that was chaired by Lothar Fritch, OsloMet. The first day was rounded off by the second keynote on "AI Research and Europe's Upcoming AI Law" by Tobias Mahler, University of Oslo. The keynote discussed the legal regulation of AI that is under development in Europe, the Artificial Intelligence Act (AIA), shedding light on whether the law, if adopted, will facilitate the creation of trustworthy AI in Europe, or whether it might limit Europe's ability to develop competitive AI systems. The keynote led to an engaging discussion in plenum, where among other things, what is defined as AI in the regulation as well as security and safety aspects seemed to interest the audience. Afterwards, the Norwegian AI Society had a short General Assembly meeting, and then the participants walked down to the Norwegian Opera and Ballet and enjoyed a good dinner at Brasserie Sanguine.

Day two started with an inspiring keynote by Kjersti Aas, Big Insight Centre for Research-based Innovation, about ongoing work at Big Insight. Examples included the application of AI and machine learning in credit scoring, anomaly detection, and detection of money laundering as well as work on explainable AI. The talk was followed by a technical session on AI in Biological Applications and Medicine, chaired by Michael Riegler, SimulaMet. The first paper of this session received the Best Paper award based on the review evaluation score. After a hearty coffee break, the event resumed with a technical session on New AI Methods, chaired by Pedro Lind, OsloMet. The event was rounded off by a final keynote by Robert Jenssen, The Arctic University of Norway. The talk presented work from the Visual Intelligence Centre for Research-based Innovation, focusing on the development of new methods for learning from limited data, e.g. semi-supervised learning, few-shot learning, and self-supervised learning, and on explainable AI – for applications ranging from fish detection to medical imaging. The main event was concluded by a short thank-you talk by co-chairs Anis Yazidi and Evi Zouganeli, OsloMet. After that, the participants could mingle over a networking buffet lunch.

Three tutorials were offered. The first one took place prior to the main event on the morning of the first day; it was entitled "Search Algorithms in AI with Python" and delivered by by Rashmi Gupta and Morten Goodwin, University of Agder. The other two tutorials took place in parallel after the end of the main event, on the afternoon of day two. The second tutorial was entitled "Goal! A practical guide to soccer video understanding" and presented by A. Cioppa, S. Giancola, A. Deliege, F. Magera, V. Somers, Le Kang, Xin Zhou, B. Ghanem, and M. Van Droogenbroeck representing Soccer Net. The third tutorial was entitled "The past, present, and future of XAI", and delivered by Kristoffer Wickstrøm, The Arctic University of Norway.

We are grateful to the Norwegian Research Council for funding the event, which did not require a fee this year. The success of the symposium would not be possible without the help of many colleagues. We would like to thank the Technical Program Committee for reviewing the papers and giving feedback to the authors. The Organizing Committee from OsloMet and SimulaMet acted, in effect, as the event Program Committee, and we would like to thank all colleagues for their commitment. We are grateful to the Artificial Intelligence Lab, the Department of Computer Science, and the Department of Mechanical, Electronics, and Chemical Engineering at OsloMet for supporting the event. We also thank the Course and Conference Centre (KK-senter) and Technical Support at OsloMet for their valuable assistance.

Last but not least, we would like to thank all participants at the symposium, including authors, speakers, keynote speakers, panelists, and session chairs – for presenting their work, engaging in discussions, actively participating in a lively exchange, and supporting the AI community.

June 2022

Evi Zouganeli
Anis Yazidi
Gustavo Mello
Pedro Lind

Organization

General Co-chairs

Evi Zouganeli   Oslo Metropolitan University, Norway
Anis Yazidi   Oslo Metropolitan University, Norway

Organizing Committee

Cise Midoglu   Simula Metropolitan, Norway
Steven Hicks   Simula Metropolitan, Norway
Trym Lindell   Oslo Metropolitan University, Norway
Ola Huse Ramstad   Norwegian University of Science and Technology, Norway

Athanasios Lentzas   Oslo Metropolitan University, Norway
Pedro Lind   Oslo Metropolitan University, Norway
Arvind Keprate   Oslo Metropolitan University, Norway
Gustavo Mello   Oslo Metropolitan University, Norway
Andrija Milojevic   Oslo Metropolitan University, Norway
Michael Riegler   Simula Metropolitan, Norway
Tiina Komulainen   Oslo Metropolitan University, Norway

Technical Program Committee

Steven Hicks   Simula Metropolitan, Norway
Cise Midoglu   Simula Metropolitan, Norway
Athanasios Lentzas   Oslo Metropolitan University, Norway
Valeria Vitelli   University of Oslo, Norway
Tom Glover   Oslo Metropolitan University, Norway
Morten Goodwin   University of Agder, Norway
Baltasar Beferull Lozano   University of Agder, Norway
Kristine Heiney   Oslo Metropolitan University, Norway
Leendert Wienhofen   Trondheim Municipality, Norway
Thu Nguyen   SINTEF, Norway
Kyrre Glette   University of Oslo, Norway
Kai Olav Ellefsen   University of Oslo, Norway
Vajira Thambawita   Simula Metropolitan, Norway
Kerstin Bach   Norwegian University of Science and Technology, Norway

Pedro Lind   Oslo Metropolitan University, Norway
Andrea T. Marheim Storås   Simula Metropolitan, Norway
Akriti Sharma   Oslo Metropolitan University, Norway
Filippo Sanfilippo   University of Agder, Norway
Rabindra Khadka   Ymail, Norway
Hårek Haugerud   Oslo Metropolitan University, Norway
Arvind Keprate   Oslo Metropolitan University, Norway
Ismail Hassan   Oslo Metropolitan University, Norway
Youcef Djenour   SINTEF, Norway
Leonardo Rydin   Oslo Metropolitan University, Norway
Michael Tarlton   Oslo Metropolitan University, Norway
Marija Slavkovik   University of Bergen, Norway

Contents

Towards New AI Methods

Robotics and Intelligent Systems

Knowledge Infused Representations Through Combination of Expert Knowledge and Original Input

Daniel Biermann[(⊠)], Morten Goodwin, and Ole-Christoffer Granmo

Centre for Artificial Intelligence Research (CAIR), Department of ICT,
University of Agder, Grimstad, Norway
daniel.biermann@uia.no

Abstract. Sophisticated applications in natural language processing, such as conversational agents, often need to be able to generalize across a range of different tasks to generate natural-feeling language. In this paper, we introduce a model that aims to improve generalizability with regard to different tasks by combining the original input with the output of a task-specific expert. Through a combination mechanism, we create a new representation that has been enriched with the information given by the expert. These enriched representations then serve as input to a downstream model. We test three different combination mechanisms in two combination paradigms and evaluate the performance of the new enriched representation in a simple encoder-decoder model. We show that even very simple combination mechanisms are able to significantly improve performance of the downstream model. This means that the encoded expert information is transported through the new enriched input representation, leading to a beneficial impact on performance within the task domain. This opens the way for exciting future endeavors such as testing performance on different task domains and the combination of multiple experts.

Keywords: Artificial neural networks · Natural language processing · Knowledge representation · Knowledge transfer

1 Introduction

In the field of natural language processing (NLP), conversational agents or chatbots are of ongoing interest. Challenges like the Amazon Alexa prize challenge[1] further incentivise research on chatbots in open-domain settings such as day-to-day conversation. A significant challenge in open-domain settings is the wide field of tasks these conversational agents encounter. For example, in a day-to-day conversation, a chatbot might need to simultaneously generate grammatically correct sentences while identifying different types of sentences (dialogue act

---

[1] https://developer.amazon.com/alexaprize.

© The Author(s) 2022
E. Zouganeli et al. (Eds.): NAIS 2022, CCIS 1650, pp. 3–15, 2022.
https://doi.org/10.1007/978-3-031-17030-0_1

classification), recognizing intent (intent classification) and answering questions (question answering).

Transfer learning is the field of using the knowledge of an intelligent agent trained in one task for another task. It is of natural interest to the field of NLP as all tasks share the underlying concept of language. This mainly shows in the practice of pre-training models on large text corpora to generate contextualized word representations, i.e. ELMo [12]. Since the inception of the Transformer model [18], the Transformer's efficiency prompted a trend in research to improve performance by pre-training Transformer-based models of rapidly increasing size on vast sets of unlabeled data and fine-tuning them for a specific task. Prominent examples are the GPT architectures [1,13,14] as well as BERT architectures (e.g. [3,9,16]) and XLNet [20]. The problem with these architectures are the massive costs of pretraining. The costs have already reached regions in which only corporations like Google, Facebook, etc. can afford to train these large models from the ground up.

Next to the pretraining-finetuning approaches, Mixture-of-Expert (MoE) and other ensemble methods are of particular interest for transfer learning. The idea behind ensemble models is to combine an ensemble of distinct experts in a way that the different experts offset the weaknesses of the other experts and elevate the overall architecture to a better and more robust performance, possibly across different tasks.

In this paper we propose a new, ensemble-based architecture that combines task-specific expert output with the initial input representation to form a new expert-information-enriched representation to serve as input for a downstream task model. Meaning, we combine the output of an expert solving a specific task with the original input word embeddings. Our model utilizes, in contrast to other ensemble models, an already trained expert whose output shape differs significantly from the original input shape. Furthermore, we explore in our proposed architecture different combination methods that are based on attention and RNNs. Additionally, we explore these methods in a dimensional- and sequential combination paradigm.

2   Related Work

The idea to combine seperate experts has been explored since the 90's [7,8]. Early renditions of MoE models used a gating function to decide which expert output is further propagated. Recent MoE research pushed the concept of sparsely-activated models such as the Switch-Transformers [5], enabling efficient models with trillions of parameters. MoE models mainly aim at creating sparse models where each incoming example is processed by different parameters, thus, possibly training different parameter sets for different tasks. This is in contrast to dense networks in which the parameters are shared for each input. Our approach differs from these MoE models in that the experts are already trained and can have different architectures and output shapes. In MoE models, the experts often have the same architecture and output shape and have to be trained.

Using ensemble models to create new word embeddings has been the subject of previous research. [10] combined different word embeddings by ordinary least squares regression and by solving the orthogonal Procrustes problem while [21] creates word meta-embeddings by combining different word embeddings via different ensemble methods. Recently, [4] employed an attention network to combine semantic lexical information of knowledge graphs and pre-trained word embeddings in an ensemble method. The method proposed in our work differs from these previous approaches. The biggest difference is that the mentioned works aimed at creating general word embeddings instead of task specific embeddings. By task-specific embeddings we mean a vector representation that is infused with the output of an expert solving a specific task. Thus, the representations generated in this work are created with specific tasks is mind. Creating task specific embeddings allows for a more flexible use of the architecture as we can tailor the experts that we choose to combine to the downstream task. Additionally, we use Transformer-base attention mechanisms to combine the original input with the expert output. Rather than creating new general word embeddings, we infuse the original word embedding with focused task-specific information in form of the output of task-specific experts.

3 Methods

3.1 Model

Fundamentally, our architecture resembles a classic encoder-decoder model. The encoder consists of the pre-trained expert and the combination mechanism, and generates the new enriched word-knowledge representation. The decoder consists of a downstream task model that is to be trained to perform its downstream task.

In the encoder, we present the input embedding to the expert which subsequently calculates the output. The original input embedding and expert output are then concatenated and passed towards the combination mechanism. The combination mechanism calculates the expert-knowledge-enriched representation that has the same dimensionality as the original input embedding. The idea of enforcing the same dimensionality is to further support the modular structure of the architecture. This way, the expert combination process can be easily interjected between the original word embedding and the downstream model without having to change the downstream model. This input embedding is then used as input for the decoder. The general structure is outlined in Fig. 1.

In general, the expert and downstream model can be arbitrary models of arbitrary tasks with the experts already trained. The expert is regarded a finished model and is NOT trained in our architecture. The idea is to be able to make use of old already trained models and available pre-trained models to improve performance of the downstream model either in the same or a different task.

In this paper, we explore the simplest case of combining 1 expert that has the same task domain as the downstream model. We choose the Context-Aware Self Attention dialogue act classifier model (CASA) [15] as an expert. Compared to the original CASA model, we only use pre-trained Glove vectors [11] as word embeddings for the expert and replace the CRF classifier with a softmax classifier with 1000 hidden units. We test different combination methods and paradigms that are described in more detail below.

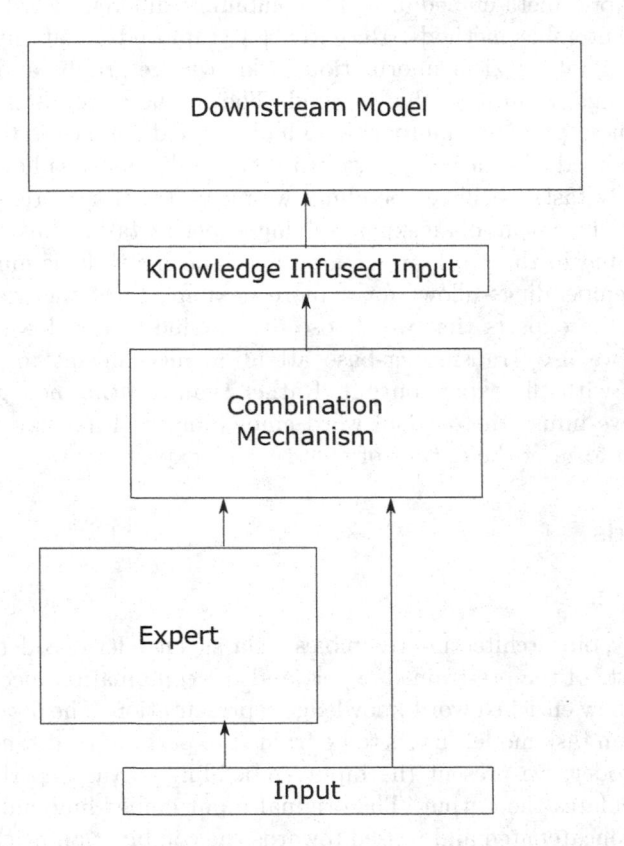

Fig. 1. Model architecture. Experts are pre-trained task-specific models. Downstream models are arbitrary, to-be-trained models. The combination mechanism combines the expert output and original input into a new enriched representation.

The downstream model consists of a single GRU (one-directional) layer [2] followed by a softmax classifier with 64 hidden units. We train the downstream model on the same task and dataset as the CASA expert.

When training the downstream model on the same task and data as the expert, we technically do not perform transfer learning as the task domains are the same. Nevertheless, by using a sophisticated, well-performing expert and a worse-performing, simple classifier we can test whether the task-knowledge infused in the enriched knowledge representation translates to a better performance in a simple model.

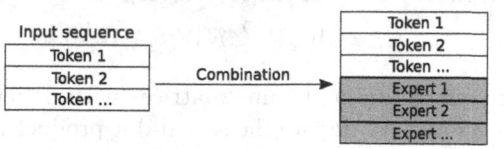

 is followed by the figure content:

Dimensional Paradigm

Sequential Paradigm

Fig. 2. Illustration of the dimensional and sequential combination paradigms.

3.2 Combination Paradigms

In our architecture we explore two different combination paradigms: Dimensional and sequential. These paradigms are illustrated in Fig. 2.

Dimensional Paradigm. In the dimensional paradigm, the expert output that has the number of classes as dimension is concatenated with the input embedding of each token in the input sequence, leading to the dimensionality $d_{emb} + d_{class}$. This concatenated vector is then presented to the combination mechanism as its input representation.

Sequential Paradigm. In the sequential paradigm, the expert output is appended to the list of tokens in the input sequence. For that, the output of the expert of dimension d_{class} is projected to the embedding dimension d_{emb} using a simple fully connected feedforward layer and added to the sequence. A sequence of length N becomes a sequence of length $N + 1$.

Thus, the combination mechanisms are presented with the challenge of reducing the dimensionality in the dimensional paradigm and reducing the sequence length in the sequential paradigm.

3.3 Combination Mechanisms

We test our model with three different combination methods. The first two mechanism are the scaled dot-product attention and multi-head attention introduced with the Transformer model [18] and the third consists of a simple recurrent network.

Mutli-head Attention. The first mechanism uses multi-head attention. Revisiting the attention definitions in [18] gives us:

$$\mathcal{A}(Q, K, V) = \text{softmax}(\frac{QK^T}{\sqrt{d_k}})V \tag{1}$$

$$\mathcal{M}(Q, K, V) = \text{Concat}(H_1, \ldots, H_h)W^O \tag{2}$$

$$H_i = \mathcal{A}(QW_i^Q, KW_i^K, VW_i^V) \tag{3}$$

where Q, K and V are query, key and value matrices with dimensionalities d_k, d_q and d_v, respectively. $\mathcal{A}$ and $\mathcal{M}$ denote the scaled-dot product and multi-head attention. The multi-head attention mechanism consists of multiple heads H_i that compute the scaled-dot product in parallel. Each head has their own Q, K and V matrices and produces outputs of dimension d_v/h with the number of heads h. The outputs are then concatenated and projected up to d_v via W^O.

In the dimensional paradigm we want d_v to be of the same dimension as the original input d_{emb} to reduce the concatenated dimensions back to the embedding dimension. While in principle the attention mechanism allows to rescale the dimension by choosing d_v, the multi-head attention requires that $d_k = d_q$ and d_v can be divided by the number of heads. This makes rescaling by d_v impracticable in our model as we can not always choose the output dimensions of our experts. For the dimensional paradigm, it is therefore beneficial to follow the general practice to set $d_k = d_q = d_v = d_{emb} + d_{class}$ and rescale by changing the dimension of W^O.

In case of the sequential paradigm, we do not want to change the dimension. We calculate the attention on the sequence $N + 1$ and drop the last sequence element.

Scaled Dot-Product Attention. Setting the number of heads in multi-head attention to $h = 1$ yields the scaled-dot product.

RNN. The third mechanism consist of a simple bi-directional GRU layer with its concatenated last hidden dimensions equaling the original embedding dimension. The hidden state after the last token in the sequence serves as the new knowledge infused representation. For the sequential paradigm, we require the RNN to be bi-directional as we have to drop the last hidden state. If the RNN were one-directional, dropping the last hidden state would also drop all the expert information.

4   Experiments

We train the downstream DA classifier model for each combination method and paradigm. The results are shown in Table 2. As baseline, we have the simple classifier and CASA model that were each trained and evaluated with the unaltered GloVe embeddings as input. Additionally, we trained combination mechanism baseline models by removing the expert from the model. The purpose of this is to get a better understanding whether any performance improvement is due to additional parameters the combination mechanism introduces to the model or the information of the expert.

Each model was trained until convergence with a patience of 30. The 5 best model iterations with regard to validation accuracy were saved. The results given in Table 2 show the averaged test accuracies.

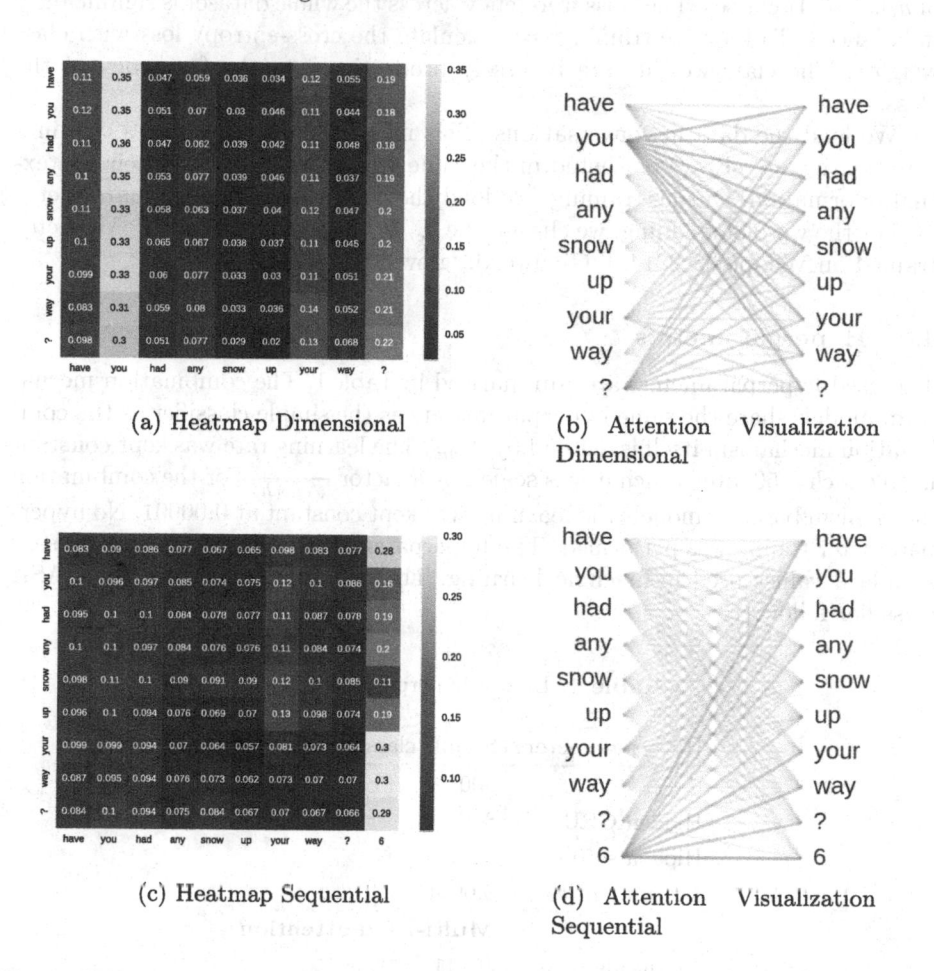

(a) Heatmap Dimensional

(b) Attention Visualization Dimensional

(c) Heatmap Sequential

(d) Attention Visualization Sequential

Fig. 3. Heatmap and attention visualization for the multi-head attention weights in both combination paradigms. The attention weights depicted have been averaged over all heads. Attention visualization created via *BertViz* [19]

4.1 Data

We train all models on the Switch-Board dialect corpus (SwDA) [6,17][2]. The dataset consists of conversations which contain sequences of sentences. We follow the train, validation and test splits given in the official paper.

After removing the non-verbal instances from the dataset, the corpus consists of $n_{class} = 41$ classes. The class frequency across the whole dataset is significantly imbalanced. To improve training, we calculate the cross-entropy loss with class weights. The class weights are inversely proportional to the frequency of the class.

We load the data in conversations. This means that the sentences within a conversation are always presented in the same order, thus retaining their contextual information. During training, we load the conversations in random order.

For the word embedding, we choose the $d_{emb} = 300$ dimensional GloVe vector trained on Wikipedia 2014 + Gigaword: 'glove.6B'.

4.2 Hyperparameters

The used hyperparameters are summarised in Table 1. The combination mechanism models share the same hyperparameters as the simple classifier as the combination mechanism itself is defined by d_{emb}. The learning rate was kept constant until epoch = 50 after which it was scaled by a factor $\frac{1}{\sqrt{epoch}}$. For the combination mechanism baseline models the learning was kept constant at 0.00001. No hyperparameter tuning was performed. The hyperparameters were chosen to represent standard values used in machine learning. The hyperparameters for the CASA classifier follow [15]

Table 1. List of hyperparameters.

Hyperparameters	Simple classifier
d_{emb}	300
Hidden GRU	8
Hidden softmax	64
Learning rate	0.0001*
	Multi-head attention
No. heads h	10/11

4.3 Results

As shown in Table 2, all combination models show a significant improvement in performance compared to the simple classifier. In addition, the combination models also show a significant improvement when compared to their baseline performance.

---

[2] This work uses the pre-cleaned dataset files provided in https://github.com/NathanDuran/Switchboard-Corpus.

Table 2. Dialogue act classification accuracies

Experiments	Test accuracy/%		
	No expert	Dimensional paradigm	Sequential paradigm
Baseline:			
Simple classifier	69.25		
CASA	75.03		
Combination mechanisms:			
Multi-head attention	70.80	75.03	74.78
Scaled dot-product attention	68.20	74.86	74.99
RNN	71.74	74.99	74.97

The simple classifier is able to reach an accuracy of 69.25. This low accuracy is expected as we chose a deliberately simple downstream model. We can also observe that the combination baseline models reach similar accuracies to the simple classifier. This solidifies that the significant performance improvement is not an artifact of the additional trainable parameters that the combination mechanism introduces. For the multi-head attention and RNN we only see small improvements to the accuracy. The performance worsens for the scaled dot-product. This suggests that a single application of the scaled dot-product might be too simple and has a detrimental effect on the information present in the pre-trained GloVe embeddings.

Nevertheless, when given outputs from an expert, all combination models in both combination paradigms significantly increase the performance and push the accuracy into the regime of the expert of ∼75%. This means that the information present in expert output is successfully infused into the new representation that we pass onto the downstream model. In case of the Multi-head attention mechanism in the dimensional paradigm, the performance equals the CASA baseline performance of 75.03%. This might indicate that the new representation has incorporated all information from the expert and carried it over to the down-stream model so that it reaches equal performance. Whether the performance of the simple downstream model fed with the expert infused representations can exceed the performance of the expert or if the expert baseline represents a performance ceiling for the downstream model is subject of future work.

Figure 3 shows the visualization of the multi-head attention weights for an example sentence for both combination paradigms. The weights are visualized as a heatmap and using the *BertViz* visualization tool.

For the dimensional paradigm, the influence of the expert output can not be made visible by attention as we infuse every token with the expert knowledge. Thus, every token carries the same expert information. Nevertheless, it can be seen that for a question, a significant part of the attention is put on the '?' token as well as the 'you' token. In attention models, we usually see more variation in the weights of single words instead of entire columns. This means that certain words carry over strongly into all new token representations. We suspect that this behavior is due to using only a single layer in the attention mechanism. Infusing all token representations with the same expert information might emphasize this effect as the combination of expert information and original token could combine into a 'universally good' or 'bad' representations. Thus, 'universally good' representations carry large weights for all new representations. The sequential attention weight heatmap does not show such a pronounced column wise attention proclivity. While the heatmap shows the significant influence of the expert output, it offers slightly more variation in weights across distinct words instead of columns (with the exception of the expert output column). This indicates that we have successfully created new word embeddings that have been infused with knowledge by paying attention to the relevant expert token. While the expert token dominates the attention weights, it can be seen that some tokens also pay attention to other tokens than the expert token. This means that the original word embedding also contributes to the new word embedding. Comparing the visualizations of the two paradigms makes the advantage of the sequential paradigms on explainability immediately obvious. While we have to speculate on what the effects of the expert are on the combination process in the dimensional paradigm, in the sequential paradigm, we can immediately see the effect of the expert output through attention itself.

Across the different paradigms the combination models perform similarly well and no clear paradigm or model outperforms the others. The multi-head attention reaches the best performance in the dimensional paradigm with an accuracy of 75.03 which is equal to the expert performance. Though, no sensible conclusion or insight can be gained from comparing the combination model accuracies as the differences between them are negligible. Apart from retaining the explainability of attention in the sequential paradigm, no clear preference of paradigms can be made with regard to performance.

4.4 Future Potential of Model

We expect that the performances will start to diverge once more sophisticated combination mechanism are employed. In our exploration, we deliberately limited our models to the simplest possible variants of the presented combination mechanisms. If the performance increase can be seen for the simplest models, it is a reasonable expectation that it will also work for more sophisticated models.

A preference of paradigm might emerge regarding computational cost as parameter space scales differently with increasing expert numbers for each paradigm. The dimensional paradigm grows faster in the trainable parameter space due to the query, key and value weight matrices that grow with increasing expert output dimensions. The sequential paradigm does not affect the query, key and value weight matrices but adds additional feedforward layers and computation calls for each expert. Nevertheless, this is an additive cost in model size for each expert instead of a multiplicative one. Thus, it can be expected that the sequential paradigm might gain an advantage when combining larger numbers of experts.

5   Conclusion

We developed a simple ensemble based architecture that creates knowledge infused representations by combining the original input with the output of a pre-trained task-specific expert. We tested this infusion process for different combination methods and paradigms. The proof of concept that this architecture is able to create knowledge infused representation opens up several exciting future research directions. We saw that knowledge infused representations improved the performance of deliberately simple downstream models. This opens exciting opportunities to simplify training of new models as we can use already trained or pre-trained models to improve the performance of simpler models. In a way, this method can be understood as a combination of an ensemble model and a pretraining-finetuning approach.

In future work, we would like to train the downstream model and expert on different tasks to investigate the architectures true transfer learning capabilities. A natural next step would be to increase the number of experts and explore the architectures ability to perform multitask learning as well as investigate the scaling behavior of the two different combination paradigms. The exploration of more sophisticated combination models is also of interest. Of particular interest is also the question whether the performance of this approach is fundamentally capped by the performance of the experts or if the combination process is able to elevate the performance beyond the experts baseline performance. In contrast to the proof of principle investigation presented in this paper, a next step is a more systematic investigation to achieve the best performance and compare it with other state-of-the-art models.

Overall, the approach of infusing already trained expert knowledge into original pre-trained representations has the potential to offer great benefits to the fields of transfer learning. The ability to combine distinct experts into expert-sets that have been selected with a specific task in mind could offer great task-specific performance gains.

References

1. Brown, T., et al.: Language models are few-shot learners. In: Larochelle, H., Ranzato, M., Hadsell, R., Balcan, M.F., Lin, H. (eds.) Advances in Neural Information Processing Systems, vol. 33, pp. 1877–1901. Curran Associates, Inc. (2020). https://proceedings.neurips.cc/paper/2020/file/1457c0d6bfcb4967418bfb8ac142f64a-Paper.pdf
2. Cho, K., et al.: Learning phrase representations using RNN encoder-decoder for statistical machine translation. arXiv preprint arXiv:1406.1078 (2014)
3. Devlin, J., Chang, M.W., Lee, K., Toutanova, K.: BERT: pre-training of deep bidirectional transformers for language understanding. arXiv preprint arXiv:1810.04805 (2018)

4. Fang, L., Luo, Y., Feng, K., Zhao, K., Hu, A.: A knowledge-enriched ensemble method for word embedding and multi-sense embedding. IEEE Trans. Knowl. Data Eng. 1 (2022). https://doi.org/10.1109/TKDE.2022.3159539

5. Fedus, W., Zoph, B., Shazeer, N.: Switch transformers: scaling to trillion parameter models with simple and efficient sparsity. arXiv preprint arXiv:2101.03961 (2021)

6. Godfrey, J., Holliman, E., McDaniel, J.: Switchboard: telephone speech corpus for research and development. In: [Proceedings] ICASSP-92: 1992 IEEE International Conference on Acoustics, Speech, and Signal Processing, vol. 1, pp. 517–520 (1992). https://doi.org/10.1109/ICASSP.1992.225858

7. Jacobs, R.A., Jordan, M.I., Nowlan, S.J., Hinton, G.E.: Adaptive mixtures of local experts. Neural Comput. **3**(1), 79–87 (1991). https://doi.org/10.1162/neco.1991.3.1.79

8. Jordan, M.I., Jacobs, R.A.: Hierarchical mixtures of experts and the EM algorithm. Neural Comput. **6**(2), 181–214 (1994)

9. Liu, Y., et al.: RoBERTa: a robustly optimized BERT pretraining approach. arXiv preprint arXiv:1907.11692 (2019)

10. Muromägi, A., Sirts, K., Laur, S.: Linear ensembles of word embedding models. arXiv preprint arXiv:1704.01419 (2017)

11. Pennington, J., Socher, R., Manning, C.D.: GloVe: global vectors for word representation. In: Proceedings of the Conference on EMNLP 2014–2014 Conference on Empirical Methods in Natural Language Processing (2014). https://doi.org/10.3115/v1/d14-1162

12. Peters, M.E., et al.: Deep contextualized word representations. In: Proceedings of the 2018 Conference of the North American Chapter of the Association for Computational Linguistics: Human Language Technologies, Volume 1 (Long Papers), pp. 2227–2237. Association for Computational Linguistics, New Orleans, Louisiana, June 2018. https://doi.org/10.18653/v1/N18-1202, https://aclanthology.org/N18-1202

13. Radford, A., Narasimhan, K., Salimans, T., Sutskever, I., et al.: Improving language understanding by generative pre-training (2018)

14. Radford, A., Wu, J., Child, R., Luan, D., Amodei, D., Sutskever, I., et al.: Language models are unsupervised multitask learners. OpenAI blog **1**(8), 9 (2019)

15. Raheja, V., Tetreault, J.: Dialogue act classification with context-aware self-attention. In: Proceedings of the 2019 Conference of the North American Chapter of the Association for Computational Linguistics: Human Language Technologies, Volume 1 (Long and Short Papers), pp. 3727–3733. Association for Computational Linguistics, Minneapolis, Minnesota, June 2019. https://doi.org/10.18653/v1/N19-1373, https://aclanthology.org/N19-1373

16. Sanh, V., Debut, L., Chaumond, J., Wolf, T.: DistilBERT, a distilled version of BERT: smaller, faster, cheaper and lighter. arXiv preprint arXiv:1910.01108 (2019)

17. Stolcke, A., et al.: Dialogue act modeling for automatic tagging and recognition of conversational speech. Comput. Linguist. **26**(3), 339–373 (2000)

18. Vaswani, A., et al.: Attention is all you need. In: Advances in Neural Information Processing Systems, pp. 5998–6008 (2017)

19. Vig, J.: A multiscale visualization of attention in the transformer model. In: Proceedings of the 57th Annual Meeting of the Association for Computational Linguistics: System Demonstrations, pp. 37–42. Association for Computational Linguistics, Florence, Italy, July 2019. https://doi.org/10.18653/v1/P19-3007, https://www.aclweb.org/anthology/P19-3007

20. Yang, Z., Dai, Z., Yang, Y., Carbonell, J., Salakhutdinov, R.R., Le, Q.V.: XLNet: generalized autoregressive pretraining for language understanding. In: Wallach, H., Larochelle, H., Beygelzimer, A., d'Alché-Buc, F., Fox, E., Garnett, R. (eds.) Advances in Neural Information Processing Systems, vol. 32. Curran Associates, Inc. (2019). https://proceedings.neurips.cc/paper/2019/file/dc6a7e655d7e5840e66733e9ee67cc69-Paper.pdf

21. Yin, W., Schütze, H.: Learning word meta-embeddings. In: Proceedings of the 54th Annual Meeting of the Association for Computational Linguistics (Volume 1: Long Papers), pp. 1351–1360 (2016)

Cognitive Robotics - Towards the Development of Next-Generation Robotics and Intelligent Systems

Evi Zouganeli[1] and Athanasios Lentzas[1,2]

[1] OsloMet - Oslo Metropolitan University, Oslo, Norway
{evizou,nasoslen}@oslomet.no
[2] Aristotle University of Thessaloniki, Thessaloniki, Greece

Abstract. In this paper we make the case for cognitive robotics, that we consider a prerequisite for next generation systems. We give a brief account of current cognition-enabled systems, and viable cognitive architectures, discuss system requirements that are currently not sufficiently addressed, and put forward our position and hypotheses for the development of next-generation, AI-enabled robotics and intelligent systems.

Keywords: Artificial cognition · Robotics · Intelligent systems

1 Introduction

Robots, and artificial systems more generally, are gradually evolving towards intelligent machines that can function autonomously in the vicinity of humans and interact directly with humans – e.g. drive our cars, work together with humans, or help us with everyday chores. Current artificial systems are good at performing relatively limited, repetitive, and well-defined tasks under specific conditions, however, anything beyond that requires human supervision. At the moment, it is not quite possible to deploy robots in new environments, broaden the scope of their operation, and allow them perform diverse tasks autonomously, as systems are not versatile, safe, nor reliable enough for that. Pre-programmed and pre-configured robots lack the ability to adapt, learn new tasks, and adjust to new domains, conditions, and missions.

Cognitive robotics is a multidisciplinary research field that has gained increased interest recently as it has become apparent that an advanced system architecture is a prerequisite for progressing from specialized "caged" systems to real-life autonomous systems [10]. Cognition encompasses the mental functions by which knowledge is acquired, retained, and used: perception, learning, memory, and thinking [25]. In humans, it encompasses processes such as judgment and evaluation, reasoning and computation, problem solving and decision making, comprehension, and production of language.

In order to realize such functionality in artificial systems, one needs to define an architecture that describes and governs these processes. Such system architectures are inspired by human cognition. They comprise the necessary modules

E. Zouganeli et al. (Eds.): NAIS 2022, CCIS 1650, pp. 16–25, 2022.
https://doi.org/10.1007/978-3-031-17030-0_2

for taking care of individual processes at many levels, and for overall system operation, as well as define the way information flow takes place for knowledge acquisition, reasoning, decision making, and detailed task execution. Ideally, a cognitive robot shall be able to abstract goals and tasks, combine and manipulate concepts, synthesize, make new plans, learn new behaviour, and execute complex tasks - abilities that at the moment only humans acquire, and lie in the core of human intelligence. Cognitive robots shall be able to interact safely and meaningfully and collaborate effectively with humans. Cognition-enabled robots should be able to infer and predict the human's task intentions and objectives, and provide appropriate assistance without being explicitly asked [24].

In this article we present work in progress, and our approach to cognitive robotics for next-generation systems. Our approach builds on two hypotheses/positions: i) Artificial Intelligence requires a robust cognitive architecture in order to become intelligent enough to be deployed in real-life systems in the vicinity of humans – interacting safely and meaningfully, and collaborating with humans. ii) Artificial cognitive systems need to encompass some of the processes of the right hemisphere of the human brain - such as holistic evaluation, holistic perception, intuition, imagination, and moral evaluation and reasoning.

We elaborate on these in this paper that is organized as follows. Firstly, we give an account of current cognition-enabled systems in Sect. 2. In Sect. 3 we outline a selection of cognitive architectures, and then proceed to presenting our approach and positions in Sect. 4. Finally, we conclude in Sect. 5.

2 Cognition-Enabled Robotics

Artificial cognitive systems are nowhere near human cognition at the moment, however, isolated narrow-scope cognitive functionality has been implemented in robotic systems to enable their operation. Cognition can be visualized as a pyramid [40] (Fig. 1) that models the flow of sensory input and information to realise cognitive functions and processes. The main cognitive processes are [3]: *Attention, Language, Learning, Memory, Perception, Thought,* and *Emotion*. Simpler processes, mostly related with behavioral elements closest to the sensory input, are at the base of the pyramid. As we move towards the top of the pyramid, more advanced and complex cognitive processes are found.

Perception is important for cognition as it provides agents with relevant information from their environment. A plethora of sensors are exploited in current systems, ranging from sensors simulating human senses (cameras, microphones etc.) [7,11], to ambient sensors and IoT devices [9]. Beyond simple object recognition, advanced perception attempts to analyze the whole scene and reason on the content of the scene [31]. Scene understanding has been used for knowledge acquisition in ambiguous situations [23].

Language-based cognitive capability has been shown to promote interaction, communication and understanding of abstract concepts [16]. Robots able to express thoughts and actions allow a better cooperation with humans [44]. An agent with the ability to summarize its actions and gain new knowledge has been demonstrated [14].

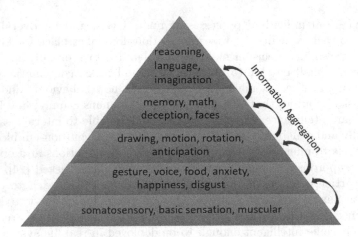

Fig. 1. Objective pyramid of cognition [40].

Learning is the core function of a cognitive system [34]. Agents can learn from expert demonstration through Imitation Learning [17], an approach that is under development. Transfer Learning is another common approach that also allows training in a simulated or protected environment [22]. Learning is currently closely woven with sensory-motor inputs and outputs, data processing, and perception, hence primarily limited to the lower layers of the cognition pyramid (Fig. 1).

The pinnacle of cognition is thinking, reasoning, decision making, planning. Reactive architectures are part of higher cognition as they affect the decision and thought process [45]. Planning and decision-making can benefit from cognition-enabled agents. Reasoning on a recognized scene allows robots to calculate an optimal path by accurately localizing itself, the goal and obstacles or dangerous areas [30]. Safety rules applied on a robot and the ability to recognize areas of potential hazard, promote a safe environment both for the robot and the humans [43]. A holistic approach to thinking with human-like cognitive reasoning and decision making processes, is far from realised, and thought processes are relatively basic at the moment.

Social robots can greatly benefit from emotional cognition [16]. Robots with the ability to recognize and express emotions (anthropomorphism) promote an easier and more effective interaction with humans [38], and robots that express empathy have been shown to help humans alter negative feelings to positive ones [5,21].

3   Cognitive Architectures

Modeling human cognition has led to the formal definition of cognitive architectures. Although first order logic approaches [20] allowed the gradual refinement of the performed actions, agents continued to lack the ability to merge new

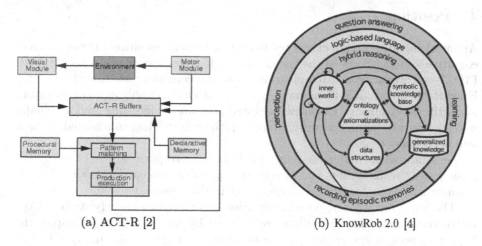

(a) ACT-R [2]   (b) KnowRob 2.0 [4]

Fig. 2. A schematic of ACT-R (a) and KnowRob 2.0 (b) architectures.

information with existing beliefs. This led to the proposal of more complex architectures. A selection of often used cognitive architectures is briefly introduced here (Fig. 2).

A commonly used architecture is ACT-R [2] where knowledge is divided based on the type of information (facts or knowledge on how to do things). Each component is accessed via a dedicated buffer, and the contents of these buffers represent the state of the world. ACT-R is based on productions, i.e. "IF" - "THEN" rules. When the current state of the world matches the precondition (using a pattern matcher module), the rule is triggered executing the relevant action. Productions, when executed, alter the state of the buffers and hence the state of the system.

A more detailed representation of human cognition is attempted by LIDA (Learning Intelligent Distribution Agent) cognitive architecture [18,19]. LIDA assumes that cognition functions on cycles with distinct phases. The first phase is perception and understanding allowing the agent to perceive the world and update the understanding of the current state. The next phase is the attention phase, where information is filtered, and the conscious content is broadcasted, followed by the action and learning phase.

The KnowRob 2.0 architecture [4] is designed specifically for robots, allowing them to perform complex tasks. At the core of the architecture are the ontologies (a subject's properties and relationships) and axioms (rules a priori true). A photorealistic representation of the environment is used for reasoning, allowing the agent to simulate its actions. Actions are stored as episodes allowing recall or knowledge transfer.

Several cognitive architectures can be considered for artificial cognition, and are extensively studied and presented by BICA [1]. In addition to the above architectures, SOAR [26], Icarus [27], and Clarion [39] are often used.

4 Position

Artificial cognitive architectures try to imitate human cognition - the epitome of cognitive systems. Some of the cognitive architectures – such as ACT-R, SOAR, LIDA – are primarily an attempt to model human cognition; whereas others – e.g. KnowRob – are inspired by human cognition but aim primarily at an architecture for artificial cognition. Cognitive architectures are progressing and gradually moving closer to human cognition, however, there is still huge uncharted ground, and a long way to go.

Semantic scene understanding, and holistic perception are only to a very basic extent realised thus far, merely at a proof-of-concept level, and there is considerable scope for further development in this area.

The importance of language in cognition was identified in early studies. Cognitive structures and capabilities are affected by language [8,37]. Despite the huge advances in speech analysis, translation, and synthesis, language is currently merely incorporated as an input/output interface in robotic systems, and is hardly included in any of the artificial cognitive processes [14,44].

Emotions have only recently been recognized as a part of cognition in humans [28,32,41] as they have previously been considered as innately hardwired into our brains. In LIDA, emotions are expressed as nodes that when triggered lead to experiencing the corresponding emotion. This is important in particular for good interaction between artificial systems and humans [13,38]. However, emotions are not incorporated in the thought process in any of the architectures or implementations, whereas in humans they often play a central role in decision making.

Currently robots are not explicitly ethical, and lack moral judgement. Ethical and moral rules have been used to that end as they can potentially affect both the acceptance of robotic applications and robotic decision making [29,33]. Norm violation may decrease human trust in an agent, therefore the agent should alter or completely discard a plan if it goes against moral values [6,12]. A fair amount of work has been done on moral reasoning and logic [15,42]. Nevertheless, moral reasoning and evaluation is not yet incorporated in cognitive architectures, neither is it an integral part of a holistic decision process. Although ethics and moral values may not be considered as part of cognition directly, in fact they play an important role in human decision making, govern human behavior, and will be instrumental for developing responsible robots.

Another relatively neglected area is artificial curiosity and imagination. While KnowRob 2.0 implements a basic form of imagination to anticipate outcomes as robots imagine the effect of their actions in their inner world representation, it is only associated to sensory-motor action and planning. Innate curiosity for exploration, global optimization, and knowledge acquisition is not explicitly accounted for in any of the reviewed architectures. This ability is critical for robots operating autonomously in unknown environments, and will allow them to effectively solve tasks even when their knowledge is not complete, and there is no human to provide the necessary information [35,36].

Moreover, current cognitive systems do not explicitly account for ingenuity. Ingenuity is the ability to employ tools or existing knowledge and use them to solve new problems in new unrelated domains. This will require complex abstraction, and synthesis of knowledge and skills. This ability will enable artificial agents to solve complex problems, and invent good solutions even when they do not have all required knowledge, sufficient experience, or the optimal tools at their disposal.

The human brain comprises two interconnected hemispheres – the left and the right – that have distinct functions and operate in different ways. The left hemisphere stands for linear thinking, detail-oriented perception, facts processing, computations, language processing, planning, logic. The right hemisphere stands for holistic thinking, holistic perception, intuitive thinking, imagination, creativity, emotional and moral evaluation. Current models of human cognition are computational in nature and represent primarily the functions of the left hemisphere. The operation and processes of the right hemisphere are by far less understood, and they are not explicitly included in the models of human cognition, let alone in robotic systems.

Our approach to attending to the above challenges in order to develop next generation robotics and intelligent systems, builds upon two main hypotheses/ positions:

i) Artificial Intelligence requires a robust cognitive architecture in order to be deployed in real-life autonomous systems in the vicinity of humans - interacting safely and meaningfully, and collaborating with humans. This hypothesis is not controversial as such, however, there is not enough awareness around this in the robotics community. Research and development in Robotics and intelligent systems has mainly targeted specific tasks and functionality - e.g. navigation, specific skill learning, etc. - rather than the overall systems architecture.

ii) In order to progress to the next level, artificial cognitive systems need to encompass some of the processes of the right hemisphere of the human brain – such as holistic evaluation, holistic perception, intuition, imagination, and moral evaluation and reasoning. This is a novel hypothesis, and needs to be proven. Our approach is to show the importance of this approach by demonstrating it in systems with superior performance.

5 Summary

In this paper we have made the case for cognitive robotics and presented our approach to next generation advanced systems. We have given an overview of human cognition, an account of cognition-enabled systems and the state of the art, and a brief outline of a selection of cognitive architectures that can lend themselves to artificial cognition. The validity of our approach remains to be demonstrated. Artificial cognitive systems are emerging, and currently at a rather early stage of development. In our opinion, they are the cornerstone towards next generation advanced robotics, the key to unlocking the potential of robots and artificial intelligence, and enabling their use in real-life applications.

References

1. Bica*ai. https://bica.ai/about/
2. Anderson, J.R., Bothell, D., Byrne, M.D., Douglass, S., Lebiere, C., Qin, Y.: An integrated theory of the mind. Psychol. Rev. **111**(4), 1036–1060 (2004)
3. Anderson, J.R.: The Architecture of Cognition. Psychology Press, New York (2009)
4. Beetz, M., Beßler, D., Haidu, A., Pomarlan, M., Bozcuoğlu, A.K., Bartels, G.: Know Rob 2.0 - a 2nd generation knowledge processing framework for cognition-enabled robotic agents. In: 2018 IEEE International Conference on Robotics and Automation (ICRA), pp. 512–519 (2018). https://doi.org/10.1109/ICRA.2018.8460964
5. Belpaeme, T., Kennedy, J., Ramachandran, A., Scassellati, B., Tanaka, F.: Social robots for education: a review. Sci. Robot. **3**(21), eaat5954 (2018). https://doi.org/10.1126/scirobotics.aat5954
6. Jackson, R.B., et al.: An integrated approach to context-sensitive moral cognition in robot cognitive architectures. In: 2021 IEEE/RSJ International Conference on Intelligent Robots and Systems (IROS), pp. 1911–1918 (2021). https://doi.org/10.1109/IROS51168.2021.9636434
7. Bonci, A., Cen Cheng, P.D., Indri, M., Nabissi, G., Sibona, F.: Human-robot perception in industrial environments: a survey. Sensors **21**(5) (2021). https://doi.org/10.3390/s21051571. https://www.mdpi.com/1424-8220/21/5/1571
8. Brown, R.W., Lenneberg, E.H.: A study in language and cognition. J. Abnorm. Soc. Psychol. **49**(3), 454–462 (1954). https://doi.org/10.1037/h0057814
9. Casagrande, F.D., Tørresen, J., Zouganeli, E.: Predicting sensor events, activities, and time of occurrence using binary sensor data from homes with older adults. IEEE Access **7**, 111012–111029 (2019). https://doi.org/10.1109/ACCESS.2019.2933994
10. Cassimatis, N.L., Bello, P., Langley, P.: Ability, breadth, and parsimony in computational models of higher-order cognition. Cogn. Sci. **32**(8), 1304–1322 (2008). https://doi.org/10.1080/03640210802455175. https://onlinelibrary.wiley.com/doi/abs/10.1080/03640210802455175
11. Charalampous, K., Kostavelis, I., Gasteratos, A.: Recent trends in social aware robot navigation: a survey. Robot. Auton. Syst. **93**, 85–104 (2017). https://doi.org/10.1016/j.robot.2017.03.002. https://www.sciencedirect.com/science/article/pii/S0921889016302287
12. Coeckelbergh, M.: How to use virtue ethics for thinking about the moral standing of social robots: a relational interpretation in terms of practices, habits, and performance. Int. J. Soc. Robot. **13**(1), 31–40 (2020). https://doi.org/10.1007/s12369-020-00707-z
13. Craig, M.J.A., Edwards, C.: Feeling for our robot overlords: perceptions of emotionally expressive social robots in initial interactions. Commun. Stud. **72**(2), 251–265 (2021). https://doi.org/10.1080/10510974.2021.1880457
14. DeChant, C., Bauer, D.: Toward robots that learn to summarize their actions in natural language: a set of tasks. In: Faust, A., Hsu, D., Neumann, G. (eds.) Proceedings of the 5th Conference on Robot Learning. Proceedings of Machine Learning Research, vol. 164, pp. 1807–1813. PMLR, 08–11 November 2022. https://proceedings.mlr.press/v164/dechant22a.html
15. Dennis, L., Fisher, M., Slavkovik, M., Webster, M.: Formal verification of ethical choices in autonomous systems. Robot. Auton. Syst. **77**, 1–14 (2016). https://doi.org/10.1016/j.robot.2015.11.012. https://www.sciencedirect.com/science/article/pii/S0921889015003000

16. Di Nuovo, A., Cangelosi, A.: Abstract concept learning in cognitive robots. Curr. Robot. Rep. **2**(1), 1–8 (2021). https://doi.org/10.1007/s43154-020-00038-x
17. Duan, Y., et al.: One-shot imitation learning. In: Guyon, I., et al. (eds.) Advances in Neural Information Processing Systems, vol. 30. Curran Associates, Inc. (2017). https://proceedings.neurips.cc/paper/2017/file/ba3866600c3540f67c1e9575e213be0a-Paper.pdf
18. Franklin, S., Madl, T., D'Mello, S., Snaider, J.: LIDA: a systems-level architecture for cognition, emotion, and learning. IEEE Trans. Auton. Ment. Dev. **6**(1), 19–41 (2014). https://doi.org/10.1016/j.bica.2016.04.003
19. Franklin, S., et al.: A LIDA cognitive model tutorial. Biologically Inspired Cogn. Architect. **16**, 105–130 (2016). https://doi.org/10.1016/j.bica.2016.04.003. https://www.sciencedirect.com/science/article/pii/S2212683X16300196
20. Gil, Y.: Learning by experimentation: incremental refinement of incomplete planning domains. In: Cohen, W.W., Hirsh, H. (eds.) Machine Learning Proceedings 1994, pp. 87–95. Morgan Kaufmann, San Francisco (1994). https://doi.org/10.1016/B978-1-55860-335-6.50019-2. https://www.sciencedirect.com/science/article/pii/B9781558603356500192
21. González-González, C.S., Violant-Holz, V., Gil-Iranzo, R.M.: Social robots in hospitals: a systematic review. Appl. Sci. **11**(13) (2021). https://doi.org/10.3390/app11135976. https://www.mdpi.com/2076-3417/11/13/5976
22. Hua, J., Zeng, L., Li, G., Ju, Z.: Learning for a robot: deep reinforcement learning, imitation learning, transfer learning. Sensors **21**(4) (2021). https://doi.org/10.3390/s21041278. https://www.mdpi.com/1424-8220/21/4/1278
23. Johnson-Roberson, M., et al.: Enhanced visual scene understanding through human-robot dialog. In: 2011 IEEE/RSJ International Conference on Intelligent Robots and Systems, pp. 3342–3348 (2011). https://doi.org/10.1109/IROS.2011.6094596
24. Kamarul Bahrin, M.A., Othman, M.F., Nor Azli, N.H., Talib, M.F.: Industry 4.0: a review on industrial automation and robotic. Jurnal Teknologi **78**(6–13) (2016). https://doi.org/10.11113/jt.v78.9285. https://journals.utm.my/jurnalteknologi/article/view/9285
25. Kihlstrom, J.F.: Unconscious cognition. In: Reference Module in Neuroscience and Biobehavioral Psychology. Elsevier (2018). https://doi.org/10.1016/B978-0-12-809324-5.21860-9. https://www.sciencedirect.com/science/article/pii/B9780128093245218609
26. Laird, J.E., Newell, A., Rosenbloom, P.S.: SOAR: an architecture for general intelligence. Artif. Intell. **33**(1), 1–64 (1987). https://doi.org/10.1016/0004-3702(87)90050-6
27. Langley, P., Choi, D.: A unified cognitive architecture for physical agents. In: Proceedings of the National Conference on Artificial Intelligence, Menlo Park, CA, vol. 21, p. 1469. AAAI Press, London/MIT Press, Cambridge (1999, 2006)
28. LeDoux, J.E., Brown, R.: A higher-order theory of emotional consciousness. Proc. Natl. Acad. Sci. **114**(10), E2016–E2025 (2017). https://doi.org/10.1073/pnas.1619316114. https://www.pnas.org/content/114/10/E2016
29. Lee, M., Ruijten, P., Frank, L., de Kort, Y., IJsselsteijn, W.: People may punish, but not blame robots. In: Proceedings of the 2021 CHI Conference on Human Factors in Computing Systems, CHI 2021. Association for Computing Machinery, New York (2021). https://doi.org/10.1145/3411764.3445284

30. Li, J., Chan, C.L., Le Chan, J., Li, Z., Wan, K.W., Yau, W.Y.: Cognitive navigation for indoor environment using floorplan. In: 2021 IEEE/RSJ International Conference on Intelligent Robots and Systems (IROS), pp. 9030–9037 (2021). https://doi.org/10.1109/IROS51168.2021.9635850

31. Metaxas, D., Daniels, Z.: Image processing neural network systems and methods with scene understanding, December 2019

32. Moore, S.C., Oaksford, M.: Emotional Cognition: From Brain to Behaviour, vol. 44. John Benjamins Publishing (2002)

33. Müller, V.C.: Is it time for robot rights? Moral status in artificial entities. Ethics Inf. Technol. **23**(4), 579–587 (2021). https://doi.org/10.1007/s10676-021-09596-w

34. Peng, X.B., Andrychowicz, M., Zaremba, W., Abbeel, P.: Sim-to-real transfer of robotic control with dynamics randomization. In: 2018 IEEE International Conference on Robotics and Automation (ICRA), pp. 3803–3810 (2018). https://doi.org/10.1109/ICRA.2018.8460528

35. Schmidhuber, J.: An on-line algorithm for dynamic reinforcement learning and planning in reactive environments. In: 1990 IJCNN, International Joint Conference on Neural Networks, vol. 2, pp. 253–258 (1990). https://doi.org/10.1109/IJCNN.1990.137723

36. Schmidhuber, J.: Developmental robotics, optimal artificial curiosity, creativity, music, and the fine arts. Connection Sci. **18**(2), 173–187 (2006). https://doi.org/10.1080/09540090600768658

37. Seleskovitch, D.: Language and cognition. In: Gerver, D., Sinaiko, H.W. (eds.) Language Interpretation and Communication. HF, vol. 6, pp. 333–341. Springer, Boston (1978). https://doi.org/10.1007/978-1-4615-9077-4_29

38. Spatola, N., Wudarczyk, O.A.: Ascribing emotions to robots: explicit and implicit attribution of emotions and perceived robot anthropomorphism. Comput. Hum. Behav. **124**, 106934 (2021). https://doi.org/10.1016/j.chb.2021.106934. https://www.sciencedirect.com/science/article/pii/S0747563221002570

39. Sun, R.: 6 the CLARION cognitive architecture: toward the mind. In: The Oxford Handbook of Cognitive Science, p. 117 (2017)

40. Taylor, P., Hobbs, J.N., Burroni, J., Siegelmann, H.T.: The global landscape of cognition: hierarchical aggregation as an organizational principle of human cortical networks and functions. Sci. Rep. **5**(1), 18112 (2015). https://doi.org/10.1038/srep18112

41. Thagard, P.: Hot Thought: Mechanisms and Applications of Emotional Cognition. MIT Press, Cambridge (2008)

42. Tolmeijer, S., Kneer, M., Sarasua, C., Christen, M., Bernstein, A.: Implementations in machine ethics: a survey. ACM Comput. Surv. **53**(6) (2021). https://doi.org/10.1145/3419633

43. Vilchis-Medina, J.L., Godary-Déjean, K., Lesire, C.: Autonomous decision-making with incomplete information and safety rules based on non-monotonic reasoning. IEEE Robot. Autom. Lett. **6**(4), 8357–8362 (2021). https://doi.org/10.1109/LRA.2021.3103048

44. Wudarczyk, O.A., et al.: Robots facilitate human language production. Sci. Rep. **11**(1), 16737 (2021). https://doi.org/10.1038/s41598-021-95645-9

45. Zhang, W., Cheng, H., Hao, L., Li, X., Liu, M., Gao, X.: An obstacle avoidance algorithm for robot manipulators based on decision-making force. Robot. Comput.-Integr. Manuf. **71**, 102114 (2021). https://doi.org/10.1016/j.rcim.2020.102114. https://www.sciencedirect.com/science/article/pii/S0736584520303240

Pattern Based Software Architecture for Predictive Maintenance

Ants Torim[✉][iD], Innar Liiv, Chahinez Ounoughi, and Sadok Ben Yahia[iD]

Tallinn University of Technology, Ehitajate tee 5, 19086 Tallinn, Estonia
`ants.torim@taltech.ee`

Abstract. Many industrial sectors are moving toward Industry Revolution (IR) 4.0. In this respect, the Internet of Things and predictive maintenance are considered the key pillars of IR 4.0. Predictive maintenance is one of the hottest trends in manufacturing where maintenance work occurs according to continuous monitoring using a healthiness check for processing equipment or instrumentation. It enables the maintenance team to have an advanced prediction of failures and allows the team to undertake timely corrective actions and decisions ahead of time. The aim of this paper is to present a smart monitoring and diagnostics system as an expert system that can alert an operator before equipment failures to prevent material and environmental damages. The main novelty and contribution of this paper is a flexible architecture of the predictive maintenance system, based on software patterns - flexible solutions to general problems. The presented conceptual model enables the integration of an expert knowledge of anticipated failures and the matrix-profile technique based anomaly detection. The results so far are encouraging.

Keywords: Predictive maintenance · Conceptual architecture · Analysis patterns · Machine learning · Time series analysis · Matrix profile

1 Introduction

The increasing capabilities of data collection mechanisms have evolved new intelligent solutions for decision-making. The burgeoning advancement in Machine Learning (ML) algorithms have yielded a tangible impact on decision-making techniques. In addition, adapting efficient management systems for maintenance work can decrease the unpredicted costs during equipment failures and shutdown periods.

Indeed, industrial equipment failure can be costly or even endanger personal safety. Therefore, moving from simple schedule-based maintenance to smart sensor-based predictive maintenance systems has become increasingly popular. However, these systems are not simple, and there are several approaches to them, including those based on expert knowledge and those based on machine learning. We propose a conceptual architecture that combines these using known solutions

© The Author(s) 2022
E. Zouganeli et al. (Eds.): NAIS 2022, CCIS 1650, pp. 26–38, 2022.
https://doi.org/10.1007/978-3-031-17030-0_3

(patterns) from the field of software engineering. The proposed architecture is based on a real-world, but anonymous industry implementation of predictive maintenance, but the approach, observations and discussions presented here are of general interest for anyone designing practical predictive maintenance systems.

The remainder of this paper is organized as follows. In Sect. 2, we present an overview of the related work about predictive maintenance models. In the next Sect. 3, we discuss the methodological contribution of our work compared to the related work and their practical applications in real-life scenarios. Next, in Sect. 3.1, we briefly present the Matrix Profile Method for Predictive Maintenance and discuss its application from the perspective of our case study. The penultimate section describes the conceptual pattern-based architecture for predictive maintenance using UML class diagrams. Finally, the conclusion and issues of future works are stated in Sect. 5.

2 Related Work

Hashemian [6] identifies eight applications of equipment condition monitoring: process optimization, personal safety, equipment health, emission monitoring, process diagnostics, equipment performance, leak detection and calibration verification. Predictive maintenance has been a field of active study [3,5,9].

In their literature review on predictive maintenance, Ran et al. [14] state the cruciality of maintenance in the industry, damage of unplanned downtime, and the capability of emerging technologies to make predictive maintenance widely accessible. They divide the approaches to predictive maintenance into three:

1. Knowledge-based approaches (Ontology-, Model- and Rule-based)
2. Traditional machine learning-based approaches (ANN, DT SVM, kNN)
3. Deep learning-based approaches (AE, CNN, RNN, DBN, GAN, etc.)

For machine learning, we make heavy use of the Matrix Profile method invented by Eamonn Keogh and Abdullah Mueen [16] which we will describe later. Our implementation is built on Python stumpy Matrix Profile library [8].

Our architecture aims to combine the rule-based approach with traditional or deep learning methods. To achieve that, we propose an architecture based on archetype and analysis patterns from software engineering. Analysis patterns were described by M. Fowler [4] as groups of concepts that represent a common construction in business modeling that may span many domains. Business archetype patterns (namely Product, Party, Order, Inventory, Quantity, and Rule), originally introduced by Arlow and Neustadt [2], are the universal information models describing the universe of discourse of businesses [13]. The archetypes and archetype patterns were further explored in the works of Piho et al. [11,12] as part of Sentry (sample entry) software for CBPG (Clinical and Biomedical Proteomics Group, Leeds Institute of Cancer and Pathology, University of Leeds). Interestingly, the Rule pattern that is fundamental for our architecture is described in these works as covering all the fundamental business requirements - What (Things), How (Processes), Where (Locations), Who

(Persons), When (Events), Why (Strategies) - of Zachman Framework [17]. To best of our knowledge the application of these patterns to the field of predictive maintenance has not been explored before. We implemented our prototype system based on this architecture through Grafana observability platform[1].

3 Matrix Profile Method for Predictive Maintenance

We make heavy use of a Matrix Profile (MP) method in our predictive maintenance system. While our architecture is general and can work with different methods, it is an effective method and an excellent example to explore the issues of time series analysis.

Time series analysis typically looks at anomalies and motifs/patterns. The basic idea of MP is to calculate the distance between pairs of sub-sequences in the time series by computing the distance between each pair. An important parameter for MP is the window size: length of sub-sequences. Despite the simplicity of a naive algorithm based on nested loops, it can take years or months to get an answer for a moderately sized time series using this method. However, using the Matrix Profile algorithms, computation time is significantly reduced. It is a relatively new time series analysis data structure invented by Eamonn Keogh [10] at the University of California Riverside, and Abdullah Mueen at the University of New Mexico [16]. A matrix profile is a vector that stores the z-normalized Euclidean distance between any sub-sequence within a time series and its nearest neighbor. This algorithm is agnostic to domains, fast, supplies an exact solution, and only requires one parameter (window size).

In Fig. 1 we show at the top a synthetic time series from a temperature sensor, which contains two sawtooth patterns and added noise. Temperature is standardized to the mean of zero and standard deviation of one. At the bottom we show the corresponding Matrix Profile values for sub-sequences of the length 640. MP values correspond to distance to nearest (most similar) sub-sequence and therefore low MP values show repeating motifs. As we can see, these identify our two sawtooth patterns. Anomalies can correspondingly be identified by large MP values as shown in Fig. 2.

Multi-dimensional MP [7] generalizes finding motifs and anomalies to multi-dimensional cases. This algorithm [15] requires careful design to minimize the additional time complexity owing to its computational complexity. In addition, although it may be tempting to look for motifs in all available dimensions (i.e., the motif must exist in all dimensions and co-occur), it has been shown that this rarely produces meaningful motifs except in the most contrived of cases [7]. An alternative strategy would be to reduce time-series dimensions to a subset of "useful" dimensions before assigning a sub-sequence as a motif.

3.1 Matrix Profile in Our Case Study

Our goal is to analyze the collected sensor data for failures in the equipment alongside detecting sensor anomalies. In our case study, we analyzed the

---

[1] https://grafana.com/grafana/.

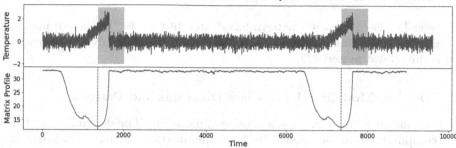

Fig. 1. Matrix profile motif detection

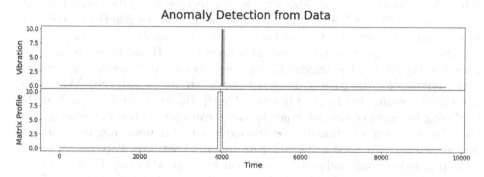

Fig. 2. Matrix profile anomaly detection

available sensor data and the correlations, adopted the MP algorithm for detecting anomalies and patterns in time-series data and extracted potential rules about sensor anomalies and device failures.

Our training dataset contained 169, 489 rows ×17 columns (sensors) collected over seven months. At the moment we have no legal rights to publish actual data from the project.

A Pearson correlation study demonstrated that the sensors' observations of the same type were highly correlated. As a result of the correlations, measurements from one sensor could be used to represent all the others of the same kind. If one goes down, the data from the other is still sufficient since their behavior is correlated.

MP is a visual method and our prototype supports visual explanations through Grafana[2] dashboard. We use both single- and multi dimensional MP. We mention shortly that we have concluded that selecting the window size is crucial for MP. We get fewer motifs whenever we go longer and vice versa. In addition, we notice anomalies at different points in the time series.

---

[2] https://grafana.com/grafana/.

4   General Architecture and Patterns

We describe the conceptual pattern-based architecture for predictive maintenance using UML class diagrams. We base this on known analysis patterns [4]
and architectural patterns [2].

4.1   Domain Modeling, UML Class Diagrams and Patterns

First, we introduce the main ideas of domain modeling. The domain is any field
that computation can be applied to [11]. Domain (Conceptual) modeling aims
to identify, detect and define the concepts from the domain. The latter are usually but not always, mirrored within the computational system. For example, in
a healthcare system, we may identify concepts like Patient, Observation, Proto-
col, etc. [4]. In the field of trading, we can identify concepts like Derivative Contract, Contract, Portfolio, Trading Package, etc. [4]. Potential concepts can be at
a higher or lower level of abstraction (Measurement vs. Blood Pressure Measurement) and be more or less relevant for certain goals (Blood Pressure Measurement
is not relevant for the goals of Trading but relevant for Healthcare). Models are
not right or wrong, but more or less valuable [4]. However, models that describe
confusing concepts or are not general enough can make extending, scaling, and
changing a system a nightmare. General models used in many different domains
and named and described in the literature are called patterns. Patterns are meant
to help with describing and proliferating good design practices [4]. They are widely
used in software engineering, but with the rapidly increasing complexity of AI systems like predictive maintenance, they should become more relevant.

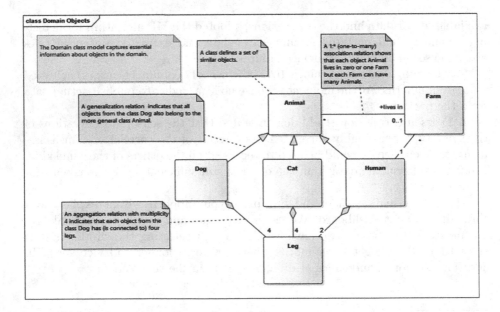

Fig. 3. Class diagram UML notation [1]

A visual way to describe domain concepts is through class diagrams of Unified Modeling Language (UML) [1]. Class diagrams can describe either domain concepts or software classes. We provide a short explanation of this notation in Fig. 3.

4.2   Patterns for Predictive Maintenance

A system of predictive maintenance should ideally combine the expert knowledge with the power of AI systems like MP to detect outliers and anomalies. Our aim is common with the field of software engineering: to protect the system from variations arising from changing user requirements.We do not want to change, reprogram and redeploy our system when user tolerance for false positives and false negatives changes, when user decides that certain indicator is not useful anymore etc. Therefore we introduce a rule interpreter that allows user/expert to add, change and delete various alert rules, controlling the behaviour of our system. We also note that these rules could apply to both actual sensor observations and machine learning anomaly/motif estimates derived from those observations. Therefore we generalize both of those into Indicators. Our general split between expert defined rules and various indicators that these rules apply to was present before we made the connection to the patterns from the field of software engineering but this connection has enabled us to clarify and generalize our approach. As it is common with patterns we have modified them to suit the needs of our specific field of predictive maintenance.

4.3   Observation and Indicator Patterns

Observation pattern (Fig. 4) was originally described by M. Fowler as follows [4]:

Observation observes some actual parameter that is either a quantity or category. Observation can, of course, be mistaken. Here we reproduce only the basic pattern which is described and extended in Fowler's book [4]. Fowler provides various extensions for the fields of Medicine and Corporate Finance.

For the field of predictive maintenance observations come from the sensors. Experts may want to use them directly in alert rules using their expert knowledge to complement machine learning estimates.

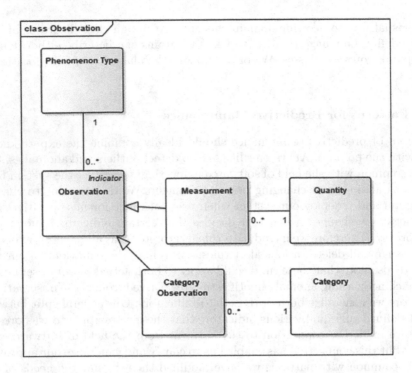

Fig. 4. Martin Fowler's Observation pattern [4]

We generalize observations from sensors and Machine Learning estimates into Indicators (Fig. 5) used for predictive maintenance analysis and alerts.Both estimates and observations are indicators.

While observation is a qualitative or quantitative statement about some measured phenomenon, an estimate is a qualitative or quantitative statement calculated based on the observations according to some method. For example, a temperature reading from some sensor is an observation, predicted likelihood of component failure is an estimate.

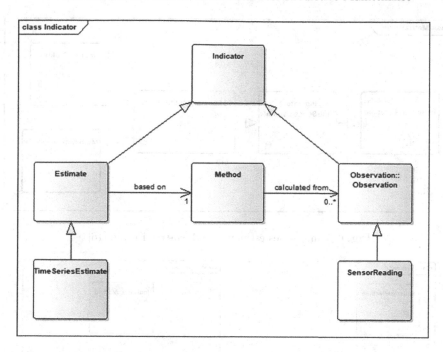

Fig. 5. Indicator pattern that extends on M. Fowler's Observation pattern [4].

4.4   Time Series Estimates Using Matrix Profile

We make heavy use of Matrix Profile and Multi-Matrix Profile estimates. They have to fit into our system of patterns which they do easily through specialization. Both are time series estimates based on a time series of observations. Both are Anomaly or Motif estimates that indicate if a particular sub-sequence of observations is a typical motif or a rare anomaly. Matrix Profile is based on a single class of observations, and Multi-Matrix Profile is based on several classes of observations. Estimating anomalies and motifs from a time series is an exceedingly useful specialization of general estimate for predictive maintenance.

4.5   Methods for Calculating Estimates

In Sect. 4.3 we mentioned a general Method that calculates Estimates from Observations. Here we introduce two specific and important subclasses of these methods. Our method for computing estimates may be realized through Queries, Pipelines, or a mix of these.

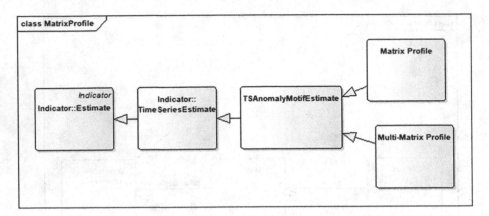

Fig. 6. Time series estimates and Matrix Profile [16]

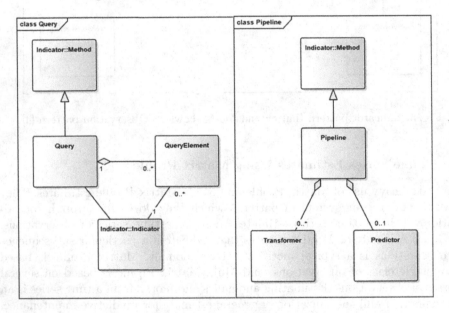

Fig. 7. Query and Pipeline methods for computing estimates.

Query methods (Fig. 7) are based on SQL-like queries from the observation database. They can also be implemented through systems like Grafana[3].

Pipeline methods (Fig. 7) transform the data through a series of transformers and finally calculate the estimate on the transformed data using a predictor. This pipeline pattern is common in machine learning, for example it is used in a popular Python machine learning library scikit-learn[4].

---

[3] https://grafana.com/grafana/.
[4] https://scikit-learn.org/stable/.

4.6   Rules and Alert Rules

We have already mentioned the need to allow experts to inject their knowledge into the system of predictive maintenance. Our solution is based on a general rule pattern well known from the field of software engineering. Rule pattern was originally described by Arlow and Neustadt [2] and has been used in various systems including laboratory management [11], etc. This pattern is central for our conceptual architecture.

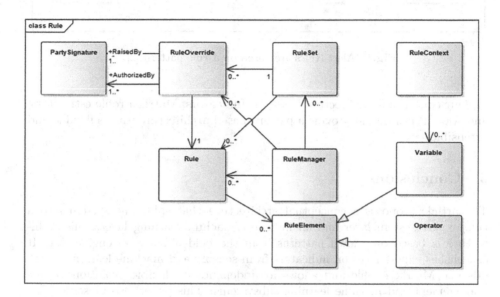

Fig. 8. Rule archetype pattern from Arlow and Neustadt [2].

As shown in Fig. 8 the original `Rule` is a sequence of `RuleElements` that can be `Variables` or `Operators`. `Variables` have values for specific `RuleContext` that could describe a date, a time, and an industrial site. If needed, a `Party` (e.g., an Expert) could override a Rule using `RuleOverride`.

Figure 9 describes our proposed Alert Rule pattern. We replace the `Rule` from Arlow and Neustadt [2] with an `Alert Rule`. `Rule Element` sets a threshold value for a particular `Indicator`. `Indicators` replace the Variables in the original pattern. For example, if temperature observation is higher than $50C$ or if Matrix Profile value is lower than 10 then the rule applies.

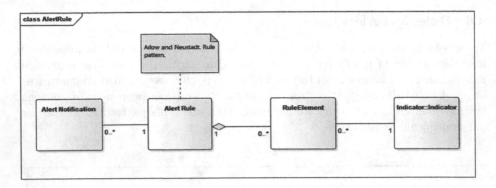

Fig. 9. Alert Rules are based on a rule pattern [2].

Our conceptual architecture based on Indicators, Matrix Profile estimators, and Alert Rules should provide a pattern-based architecture that is flexible and extensible.

5   Conclusions

The article proposes a conceptual architecture that splits the system into a rule/expert system layer and an indicator/machine learning layer. This architecture is based on known patterns from the field of software engineering. It establishes expert rules on indicators from sensors and machine learning methods like Matrix Profile and allows for independent, flexible evolution of rule management and machine learning subsystems. This paper also presented one potential set of technologies to implement such conceptual architecture, using Grafana open observability platform, Python's stumpy framework [8] for Matrix Profile. To the best of our knowledge the application of Rule and Observation patterns in our predictive maintenance architecture is a novel contribution.

We have already started building a scalable near-real-time platform to detect underperformance and uptake the proactive maintenance activities. We use the most cutting-edge techniques from machine/Deep learning and big data fields for that purpose.

The technical impact will be manifested through increased innovation facilitated by new AI solutions. The architecture of near-real-time management tool offers some distinctive features :

1. **Velocity challenge:** Provides a near real-time accurate classification of data collected (and aggregated) from multiple sources (sensors, images, videos).
2. **Zero-delay challenge:** The early detection of underperformance is pivotal as it may have dramatic consequences.
3. **Scalability:** Built using the open-source big data platform APACHE-SPARK; on top of it stands the most scalable event streaming platform APACHE-KAFKA (High throughput and availability).

References

1. About the Unified Modeling Language Specification Version 2.5.1. https://www. omg.org/spec/UML/2.5.1
2. Arlow, J., Neustadt, I.: Enterprise Patterns and MDA: Building Better Software with Archetype Patterns and UML. Addison-Wesley Professional (Dec 2003), google-Books-ID: _fSVKDn7v04C
3. Cachada, A., et al.: Maintenance 4.0: intelligent and predictive maintenance system architecture. In: 2018 IEEE 23rd International Conference on Emerging Technologies and Factory Automation (ETFA), vol. 1, pp. 139–146, September 2018. https://doi.org/10.1109/ETFA.2018.8502489, iSSN: 1946-0759
4. Fowler, M.: Analysis Patterns: Reusable Object Models. Addison-Wesley Professional (1997). google-Books-ID: 4V8pZmpwmBYC
5. Groba, C., Cech, S., Rosenthal, F., Gossling, A.: Architecture of a predictive maintenance framework. In: 6th International Conference on Computer Information Systems and Industrial Management Applications (CISIM 2007), pp. 59–64, June 2007. https://doi.org/10.1109/CISIM.2007.14
6. Hashemian, H.M.: State-of-the-art predictive maintenance techniques. IEEE Trans. Instrum. Measur. **60**(1), 226–236, January 2011. https://doi.org/10.1109/TIM. 2010.2047662, Conference Name: IEEE Transactions on Instrumentation and Measurement
7. Law, S.: Part 10: Discovering Multidimensional Time Series Motifs, May 2022. https://towardsdatascience.com/part-10-discovering-multidimensional-time-serie s-motifs-45da53b594bb
8. Law, S.M.: Stumpy: a powerful and scalable python library for time series data mining. J. Open Source Softw. **4**(39), 1504 (2019)
9. Motaghare, O., Pillai, A.S., Ramachandran, K.: Predictive maintenance architecture. In: 2018 IEEE International Conference on Computational Intelligence and Computing Research (ICCIC), pp. 1–4, December 2018. https://doi.org/10.1109/ICCIC.2018.8782406, iSSN: 2473-943X
10. Patel, P., Keogh, E., Lin, J., Lonardi, S.: Mining motifs in massive time series databases. In: 2002 IEEE International Conference on Data Mining, 2002. Proceedings, pp. 370–377, December 2002. https://doi.org/10.1109/ICDM.2002.1183925
11. Piho, G.: Archetypes based techniques for development of domains. Requirements and Software. Towards LIMS Software Factory, Tallinn (2011)
12. Piho, G., Tepandi, J., Roost, M.: Domain analysis with archetype patterns based Zachman Framework for enterprise architecture. In: 2010 International Symposium on Information Technology, vol. 3, pp. 1351–1356, June 2010. https://doi.org/10. 1109/ITSIM.2010.5561641, iSSN: 2155-899X
13. Piho, G., Tepandi, J., Thompson, D., Woerner, A., Parman, M.: Business archetypes and archetype patterns from the HL7 RIM and openEHR RM perspectives: towards interoperability and evolution of healthcare models and software systems. Procedia Comput. Sci. **63**, 553–560 (2015). https://doi. org/10.1016/j.procs.2015.08.384, https://www.sciencedirect.com/science/article/ pii/S1877050915025193
14. Ran, Y., Zhou, X., Lin, P., Wen, Y., Deng, R.: A survey of predictive maintenance: systems, purposes and approaches. arXiv:1912.07383 [cs, eess] (December 2019), arXiv: 1912.07383
15. Yeh, C.C.M., Kavantzas, N., Keogh, E.: Matrix Profile VI: Meaningful Multidimensional Motif Discovery, pp. 565–574, November 2017. https://doi.org/10.1109/ICDM.2017.66

16. Yeh, C.C.M., et al.: Matrix profile I: all pairs similarity joins for time series: a unifying view that includes motifs, discords and shapelets. In: 2016 IEEE 16th International Conference on Data Mining (ICDM), pp. 1317–1322 (2016). https://doi.org/10.1109/ICDM.2016.0179
17. Zachman, J.A.: The Zachman Framework for Enterprise Architecture. Primer for Enterprise Engineering and Manufacturing.[si]: Zachman International (2003)

AI in Cyber and Digital Sphere

An Overview of Artificial Intelligence Used in Malware

Lothar Fritsch$^{(\boxtimes)}$, Aws Jaber , and Anis Yazidi

Department of Information Technology, Faculty of Technology, Art and Design,
Oslo Metropolitan University, Oslo, Norway
{lotharfr,awsalzar,anisy}@oslomet.no
https://www.oslomet.no

Abstract. Artificial intelligence (AI) and machine learning (ML) methods are increasingly adopted in cyberattacks. AI supports the establishment of covert channels, as well as the obfuscation of malware. Additionally, AI results in new forms of phishing attacks and enables hard-to-detect cyber-physical sabotage. Malware creators increasingly deploy AI and ML methods to improve their attack's capabilities. Defenders must therefore expect unconventional malware with new, sophisticated and changing features and functions. AI's potential for automation of complex tasks serves as a challenge in the face of defensive deployment of anti-malware AI techniques. This article summarizes the state of the art in AI-enhanced malware and the evasion and attack techniques it uses against AI-supported defensive systems. Our findings include articles describing targeted attacks against AI detection functions, advanced payload obfuscation techniques, evasion of networked communication with AI methods, malware for unsupervised-learning-based cyber-physical sabotage, decentralized botnet control using swarm intelligence and the concealment of malware payloads within neural networks that fulfill other purposes.

Keywords: Information security · Artificial intelligence · Malware · Steganography · Covert channels · Machine learning · Adverse artificial intelligence

1 Introduction

In recent years, AI has been increasingly adopted as part of cyber attack methods. The application of AI on the defender's side has been successfully used in intrusion detection systems and is widely deployed in network filtering, phishing protection, and botnet control. However, the enhancement of the capabilities of malware with the help of AI methods is a relatively recent development.

This article presents the result of a literature survey mapping the state of AI-powered malware. The salient aims of this survey is to map AI-enhanced attacks carried out by malware, to identify malware types that conceal themselves from detection using AI techniques, to get a better understanding of the maturity

E. Zouganeli et al. (Eds.): NAIS 2022, CCIS 1650, pp. 41–51, 2022.
https://doi.org/10.1007/978-3-031-17030-0_4

of those attacks, and to identify the algorithms and methods involved in those attacks (Fig. 1 and Table 1).

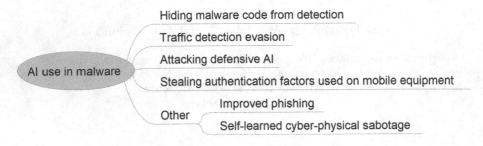

Fig. 1. Uses of AI in malware.

Table 1. Table of acronyms

Acronym	Expanded
AI	Artificial Intelligence
ANN	Artificial Neural Networks
CC	Command and Control
DNN	Deep Neural Network
GAN	Generative Adversarial Neural Networks
ML	Machine Learning

2 Literature Review on AI-Powered Malware

2.1 Literature Search

For assessing the state of the art in AI-supported malware, we performed a literature search using the Google Scholar database of scientific publications. We defined the search criteria as follows. Search keywords were *malware, artificial intelligence, machine learning* combined with *offensive, adversarial, attack, network security, information security*. The resulting articles were checked against inclusion criteria. The resulting article set was then snowballed backward and forward [36]. We limited the backward snowballing range by cutting off snowballing for articles older than 2010. Eligible forms of publications were *scientific articles, conference presentation, pre-prints and technical reports*. For inclusion, articles needed to contain *descriptions of malware functionality based on machine learning or AI functionality*. Both *survey articles* as well as *articles describing demonstrators or specific malware* were included. Our final set of articles were 37 articles.

After collecting the articles, we classified the articles into categories reflecting the specific malware functionality enhanced with AI techniques. Our findings are summarized below.

2.2 Findings

Among the deployed technologies are authentication factor extraction, generation of phishing and malware domain names, adaptive generation of phishing-e-mail, direct attacks against malware detection (code obfuscation, model poisoning) and intrusion detection (generative traffic imitation as well as AI model poisoning attacks). In addition, we found publications describing the successful parsing and controlling of graphical application user interfaces (GUIs). Finally, self-learning malware aimed at sabotage of or through cyber-physical systems was found. In particular, the evasion of detection of malware and the exfiltration of information through covert channels have been recently used in AI-powered malware.

The establishment of covert channels is an established practice for malware distribution, command and control of malware agents, and information exfiltration. Such covert channels intend to bypass intrusion detection, malware detection, and anomaly detection systems.

2.3 Surveys

Our search found 13 survey articles that were either fully or partially present knowledge about AI-enhanced malware (see Table 2). We found ten surveys, two taxonomic articles, and one anecdotal collection of AI attack use cases.

The surveys focus on different perspectives of the offensive use of AI against information security in malware:

- Surveys that summarize the use of AI-enhanced malware for different purposes: Probing, scanning, spoofing, misdirection, execution, or bypass;
- Summary of methods and algorithms used for direct attacks against a defender's AI and ML systems, e.g. evasion attacks, model poisoning, adverse samples.
- Surveys of malware improvements concerning exfiltration, code permutation, automation, and reverse engineering with AI;
- Surveys on generative networks used for attack and defense;
- Survey on stegomalware, where AI is used to hide malware in images;
- Several surveys taxonomiz offensive AI in malware into categories: intelligence, evasion, target selection, attack automation, generating malware, hiding malware, combining attack techniques, adjusting features, automating attacks at high speed.

Table 2. Surveys and taxonomies

Paper	Malware class (purpose)	AI capability used (algorithm, goal)
[18]	Malicious uses of AI: Probe, Scan, Spoof, Flood, Misdirect, Execute, Bypass	Survey with both use cases, algorithms mentioned and references to prototypes
[34]	AI Exfiltration and intelligent malware background	Various sources for exfiltration, permutation of code, reverse engineering of functionality, automation
[17]	Attack opportunities for AI attacks in COVID-19 themed fraud	Attack cases and known implementations
[25, 26]	Systematic taxonomy of adversarial attacks against ML	Detailed analysis of attack goals, algorithms, threat model
[21]	Attacks on ML in Training and Inference phase	Poisoning, Evasion, Impersonation, Inversion, Summary of algorithms
[3]	Use of generative networks in attack and defense	Describes various application areas and attacks
[5]	Stegomalware - hiding malware in images (evasion)	Large survey over algorithms and their performance
[11]	Weaponizing code, use cases and risks	Issues of control, deployment, Proliferation of AI cyberweapons
[32]	AI techniques in malware	Evasion, Autonomy, Anti-AI, Bio-inspired
[38]	AI-empowered cyberattacks	Including malware capabilities and references
[20]	Speculative taxonomy of malware with AI	Various purposes: intelligence, Evasion, Target selection, Attack automation, Generating malware, Hiding malware, Combining attack techniques, Adjusting features, Automating attacks at high speed,
[10]	Anecdotal enumeration of AI attack use cases	No algorithms or methods mentioned

2.4   AI-Enabled Attacks on Authentication Factors

Four articles described attacks against authentication factors on mobile devices'. The devices' sensors (microphone, accelerometer) were used in combination with AI models with the intention of extracting PINs, passwords, and patterns. The articles are listed in Table 3. We found two categories of AI weaponization against authentication factors:

– Prediction of PINs and passwords using accelerometer sensors in phones and wearables;
– Analysis of phone microphone records to generate PIN and credit card numbers from touch tones;

Table 3. Password extraction or prediction

Paper	Malware class (purpose)	AI capability used (algorithm, goal)
[27]	Smartphone PIN prediction using smartwatch motion sensors	Random forest classifier
[28]	Soundcomber: Extraction of PIN and credit card numbers through mobile phone microphones	Speech and touchtone analysis based on model
[30]	PIN skimmer: prediction of PIN codes using smartphone sensors	Prediction model in mobile malware
[23]	Password extraction through mobile device accelerometer	Classifier, random forest, 46 features

2.5 Techniques for Hiding Malware Code from Detection

AI is frequently used for hiding malware code from detection. The eleven articles listed in Table 4 show these approaches:

1. Hiding malware code as payload inside AI models fulfilling other functions, e.g., neural networks for face recognition;
2. Code perturbation for detection evasion automated with learning algorithms and prediction;
3. Code generation with Generative Adversarial Networks that blackbox-test filters for successful evasion;
4. Attacking AI systems for malware detection through attacks against the learning function (presentation of malicious samples, model poisoning, gradient attacks);
5. Sandbox detection in order to evade detection in sandboxed environments.

Table 4. Code detection evasion

Paper	Malware class (purpose)	AI capability used (algorithm, goal)
[15]	Hiding malware in Deep Neural Network (DNN)	Demonstrates how malware bytes can be hidden in neural networks without loss of DNN performance
[35]	EvilModel 2.0: Hiding malware - systematic experiments on model performance	Neural networks
[31]	Deeplocker: Hiding and targeting malware in neural networks	DNN, evasion, personalized biometric trigger
[12, 13]	Proposal: Improved malware performance; some background on vulnerability prediction	Unsupervised learning, learning and evasion techniques are suggested (decision tree, Bayes)
[15]	Malware code obfuscation	A Turing-complete evolutionary algorithm able to generate completely new code, evaluated with Jacquard Similarity
[16]	Generating malware that bypasses malware filter	Generative Adversarial Network (GAN) with a substitute detector to fit the black-box malware detection system
[1]	Malware binary detection evasion	Prototyped code obfuscation with reinforcement learning tested against antivirus software
[19]	Detection evasion through gradient attack	Model poisoning in DNN through malicious samples
[6]	Evasion of malware detection based on OS API calls	Feature set manipulation using bidirectional feature selection, forward feature addition
[24]	Sandbox detection from within malware	Two methods using decision trees and neural networks

2.6   Evading Network Traffic Detection

Hiding malware's communication traffic is published in four articles (see Table 5). AI and specifically unsupervised learning, is deployed against intrusion detection systems. Demonstrators described in the articles hide probing and infiltration traffic as well as command and control traffic. One noteworthy article deploys swarm intelligence in order to coordinate Botnet agents without a centralized command server.

Table 5. Evasion of network intrusion detection

Paper	Malware class (purpose)	AI capability used (algorithm, goal)
[14]	Evasion: Perturbation of network traffic against learning IDS	Stochastic approximation and adaptive random search
[22]	Evasion of malware command and control traffic from detection	Generated adversarial samples
[33]	Evasion of network intrusion detection	GANs perturbate traffic patterns
[4]	Botnet coordination without hierarchical CC servers	Multi-agent-swarm using stigmeric communication model

2.7   Other AI Deployment

Table 6 lists the miscellaneous applications of AI in the malware context. We found six articles describing enhanced capabilities in the areas of phishing, Application control and sabotage. AI is used for creating phishing domain names that evade detection in anti-phishing-systems. One spear phishing demonstrator extracts social media sentiments using AI in order to turn them into phishing e-mail-text, learning which topics are susceptible of currently provoking most reaction from the targets.

An interesting application of image recognition is malware that can understand graphical user interface elements with AI with the goal of finding out which GUI elements it can control to execute functionality.

Finally, undetectable sabotage in cyber-physical systems has been demonstrated in two cases: i) A surgical robot which - injected with malware - can learn how to modify its actions similar to normal actions in order to hurt patients. ii) The second demonstration case showed how to AI can learn to manipulate smart house technology in ways that will be hard to notice. Such AI-empowered sabotage is envisioned to be used against variable targets, dramatically leveraging the preparation effort of cyber sabotage.

3   Discussion of Findings

The presented survey investigated the use of artificial intelligence (AI) techniques and of machine learning (ML) for the improvement of malware capabilities. We found surveys and literature that describe a variety of deployments of AI in the malware context:

Table 6. Miscellaneous AI applications in malware

Paper	Malware class (purpose)	AI capability used (algorithm, goal)
[29]	Spear phishing on social media	Phishing text generation with GAN models learning trendy topics from social media
[2]	Generation of undetectable phishing domain URLs (evasion)	GAN to construct a deep learning based Domain generation algorithms (DGA) that is designed to intentionally bypass a deep learning based detector.
[37]	Malware controlling GUI elements	AI-based object recognition
[7]	Cyber-physical attacks through hidden malicious behavior	Self-learning attack strategies, disguising, failure injection
[8]	Demonstrator: surgery robot with hidden malicious behavior	Failure injection, learning, disguising
[9]	Malware attacks on surgical robot and home automation	Statistical learning, payload generation and attack planning

- Direct sabotage of defending AI or ML algorithms;
- Detection evasion through intelligent code perturbation techniques;
- Detection evasion through learning of traffic patterns in case of scanning systems, communication or connection to command and control infrastructures;
- Black-box-techniques bypassing intrusion detection using generative networks and unsupervised learning;
- Direct attacks predicting passwords, PIN codes;
- Automatic interpretation of user interfaces for application control;
- Self-learning system behavior for undetected automated cyber-physical sabotage;
- Botnet coordination with swarm intelligence, removing need for command and control servers;
- Sandbox detection and evasion with neural networks;
- Hiding malware within images or neural networks.

We conclude that AI deployed to either improve or hide malware poses a considerable threat to malware detection. Code obfuscation, code behavior adaption, as well as learned communication detection evasion potentially bypass existing malware detection techniques.

Offensive deployment of AI within malware improves malware performance, including methods such as selection of targets, extracting authentication factors, enabling the automated and fast generation of highly efficient Phishing messages, and swarm-coordinated action planning.

We consider AI-enhanced malware to be a serious risk for information security, which should be thoroughly investigated.

Acknowledgements. The work leading to this article was partially sponsored by OsloMET's AI Lab.

References

1. Anderson, H.S., Kharkar, A., Filar, B., Evans, D., Roth, P.: Learning to evade static PE machine learning malware models via reinforcement learning. arXiv:1801.08917 [cs] (2018)
2. Anderson, H.S., Woodbridge, J., Filar, B.: DeepDGA: adversarially-tuned domain generation and detection, pp. 13–21 (2016). https://doi.org/10.1145/2996758.2996767
3. Bauer, L.A., Bindschaedler, V.: Generative models for security: attacks, defenses, and opportunities (2021). http://arxiv.org/abs/2107.10139
4. Castiglione, A., De Prisco, R., De Santis, A., Fiore, U., Palmieri, F.: A botnet-based command and control approach relying on swarm intelligence. J. Netw. Comput. Appl. **38**, 22–33 (2014). https://www.sciencedirect.com/science/article/pii/S1084804513001161
5. Chaganti, R., Ravi, V., Alazab, M., Pham, T.D.: Stegomalware: a systematic survey of malwarehiding and detection in images, machine learningmodels and research challenges (2021). https://arxiv.org/abs/2110.02504v1
6. Chen, L., Ye, Y., Bourlai, T.: Adversarial machine learning in malware detection: arms race between evasion attack and defense. In: 2017 European Intelligence and Security Informatics Conference (EISIC), pp. 99–106 (2017)
7. Chung, K., Kalbarczyk, Z.T., Iyer, R.K.: Availability attacks on computing systems through alteration of environmental control: smart malware approach. In: ICCPS 2019: ACM/IEEE 10th International Conference on Cyber-Physical Systems, pp. 1–12 (2019). https://doi.org/10.1145/3302509.3311041
8. Chung, K., et al.: Smart malware that uses leaked control data of robotic applications: the case of Raven-II surgical robots. In: 22nd International Symposium on Research in Attacks, Intrusions and Defenses (RAID 2019), pp. 337–351 (2019). https://www.usenix.org/conference/raid2019/presentation/chung
9. Chung, K., et al.: Machine learning in the hands of a malicious adversary: a near future if not reality. In: Game Theory and Machine Learning for Cyber Security, pp. 289–316 (2021). https://onlinelibrary.wiley.com/doi/abs/10.1002/9781119723950.ch15
10. CISOMAG: artificial intelligence as security solution and weaponization by hackers. CISO MAG Cyber Security Magazine (2019). https://cisomag.eccouncil.org/hackers-using-ai/
11. Cobb, S., Lee, A.: Malware is called malicious for a reason: the risks of weaponizing code. In: 2014 6th International Conference on Cyber Conflict (CyCon 2014), pp. 71–84 (2014)
12. Easttom, C.: Integrating machine learning algorithms in the engineering of weaponized malware. In: ECIAIR 2019, European Conference on the Impact of Artificial Intelligence and Robotics, pp. 113–121 (2019)
13. Easttom, C.: A methodological approach to weaponizing machine learning. In: The 2019 International Conference, pp. 1–5 (2019). http://dl.acm.org/citation.cfm?doid=3358331.3358376
14. Fladby, T., Haugerud, H., Nichele, S., Begnum, K., Yazidi, A.: Evading a machine learning-based intrusion detection system through adversarial perturbations, pp. 161–166 (2020). https://doi.org/10.1145/3400286.3418252
15. Gaudesi, M., Marcelli, A., Sanchez, E., Squillero, G., Tonda, A.: Malware obfuscation through evolutionary packers, pp. 757–758 (2015). https://doi.org/10.1145/2739482.2764940

16. Hu, W., Tan, Y.: Generating adversarial malware examples for black-box attacks based on GAN (2017). http://arxiv.org/abs/1702.05983

17. Jaber, A.N., Fritsch, L.: COVID-19 and global increases in cybersecurity attacks: review of possible adverse artificial intelligence attacks. In: 2021 25th International Computer Science and Engineering Conference (ICSEC), pp. 434–442, November 2021. https://doi.org/10.1109/ICSEC53205.2021.9684603

18. Kamoun, F., Iqbal, F., Esseghir, M.A., Baker, T.: AI and machine learning: a mixed blessing for cybersecurity. In: 2020 International Symposium on Networks, Computers and Communications (ISNCC), pp. 1–7 (2020)

19. Kolosnjaji, B., et al.: Adversarial malware binaries: evading deep learning for malware detection in executables. In: 2018 26th European Signal Processing Conference (EUSIPCO), pp. 533–537, September 2018. https://doi.org/10.23919/EUSIPCO.2018.8553214

20. Kubovič, O., Košinár, P., Jánošík, J.: Can artificial intelligence power future malware? Technical report, ESET (2018)

21. Liu, Q., Li, P., Zhao, W., Cai, W., Yu, S., Leung, V.C.M.: A survey on security threats and defensive techniques of machine learning: a data driven view. IEEE Access 6, 12103–12117 (2018)

22. Novo, C., Morla, R.: Flow-based detection and proxy-based evasion of encrypted malware C2 traffic, pp. 83–91 (2020). https://doi.org/10.1145/3411508.3421379

23. Owusu, E., Han, J., Das, S., Perrig, A., Zhang, J.: Accessory: password inference using accelerometers on smartphones, pp. 1–6 (2012). https://doi.org/10.1145/2162081.2162095

24. Pearce, W., Landers, N., Fulda, N.: Machine learning for offensive security: sandbox classification using decision trees and artificial neural networks. In: Arai, K., Kapoor, S., Bhatia, R. (eds.) SAI 2020. AISC, vol. 1228, pp. 263–280. Springer, Cham (2020). https://doi.org/10.1007/978-3-030-52249-0_18

25. Rosenberg, I., Shabtai, A., Elovici, Y., Rokach, L.: Adversarial machine learning attacks and defense methods in the cyber security domain. ACM Comput. Surv. 54(5), 108:1–108:36 (2021). https://doi.org/10.1145/3453158

26. Rosenberg, I., Shabtai, A., Elovici, Y., Rokach, L.: Adversarial machine learning attacks and defense methods in the cyber security domain - supplementary material. ACM Comput. Surv. 54(5), 1–36 (2021). https://doi.org/10.1145/3453158

27. Sarkisyan, A., Debbiny, R., Nahapetian, A.: WristSnoop: smartphone pins prediction using smartwatch motion sensors. In: 2015 IEEE International Workshop on Information Forensics and Security (WIFS), pp. 1–6 (2015)

28. Schlegel, R., Kapadia, A., Wang, X.: Soundcomber: a stealthy and context-aware sound trojan for smartphones. In: Proceedings of the Network and Distributed System Security Symposium (NDSS) (2011)

29. Seymour, J., Tully, P.: Generative models for spear phishing posts on social media. Technical report, 31st Conference on Neural Information Processing Systems (NIPS 2017), Long Beach, CA, USA (2018). http://arxiv.org/abs/1802.05196

30. Simon, L., Anderson, R.: PIN skimmer: inferring pins through the camera and microphone, pp. 67–78 (2013). https://doi.org/10.1145/2516760.2516770

31. Stoecklin, M.: DeepLocker: how AI can power a stealthy new breed of malware. Technical report, IBM (2018). https://securityintelligence.com/deeplocker-how-ai-can-power-a-stealthy-new-breed-of-malware/

32. Thanh, C.T., Zelinka, I.: A survey on artificial intelligence in malware as next-generation threats. Mendel 25(2), 27–34 (2019). https://doi.org/10.13164/mendel.2019.2.027. https://mendel-journal.org/index.php/mendel/article/view/105

33. Usama, M., Asim, M., Latif, S., Qadir, J., Ala-Al-Fuqaha: Generative adversarial networks for launching and thwarting adversarial attacks on network intrusion detection systems. In: 2019 15th International Wireless Communications Mobile Computing Conference (IWCMC), pp. 78–83 (2019)
34. Varney, A.: Analysis of the impact of artificial intelligence to cybersecurity and protected digital ecosystems. Technical report, October 2021
35. Wang, Z., Liu, C., Cui, X., Yin, J.: EvilModel 2.0: hiding malware inside of neural network models. arXiv:2109.04344 [cs] (2021)
36. Wohlin, C.: Guidelines for snowballing in systematic literature studies and a replication in software engineering. In: Proceedings of the 18th International Conference on Evaluation and Assessment in Software Engineering, EASE 2014, pp. 1–10. Association for Computing Machinery, New York, May 2014. https://doi.org/10.1145/2601248.2601268
37. Yu, N., Tuttle, Z., Thurnau, C.J., Mireku, E.: AI-powered GUI attack and its defensive methods, pp. 79–86 (2020). https://doi.org/10.1145/3374135.3385270
38. Zouave, E., Gustafsson, T., Bruce, M., Colde, K.: Artificially intelligent cyberattacks. Technical report, FOI-R-4947-SE, Totalförsvarets forskningsinstitut FOI, March 2020

Fake News Detection by Weakly Supervised Learning Based on Content Features

Özlem Özgöbek[1]([✉]), Benjamin Kille[1], Anja Rosvold From[2],
and Ingvild Unander Netland[3]

[1] Norwegian University of Science and Technology, Trondheim, Norway
{ozlem.ozgobek,benjamin.u.kille}@ntnu.no
[2] Bredvid AS, Oslo, Norway
[3] Kantega AS, Oslo, Norway

Abstract. Fake news, defined as the publication of false information, either unintentional or with the intent to deceive or harm, is one of the important issues that affects today's digital society significantly. All around the world, journalists and fact checking organizations are trying to fight this problem manually. However, fighting fake news is a time-sensitive task. Once leaked, fake news spreads fast and its impact on society increases. Because of the complex and dynamic nature of news, applying artificial intelligence methods to address the automatic detection of fake news is a challenging task. This work explores the use of weak supervised learning for fake news detection by using only the content of news articles. This is particularly important when the contextual information is not available or difficult to obtain quickly. To our knowledge, this is the first work which uses a content-based approach in weak supervised learning without the use of any contextual information for fake news detection. We propose an architecture that generates weak labels. We explore the effect of using weak labels for fake news detection with five different machine learning models. We demonstrate that weakly supervised learning is an effective approach to the automated detection of fake news in the absence of high quality labels.

Keywords: Fake news detection · Disinformation · Weakly supervised learning · Content features

1 Introduction

The spread of fake news is not a new problem. However, with the advancement of the internet and social media, it has become a growing problem [32]. Fast and uncontrolled spread of fake news can affect society in many ways, including ideological polarization [24] and psychological bias [28]. During the Covid-19 pandemic, we have experienced how problematic the situation can be globally [7, 20]. Despite the ongoing efforts for developing automated fake news detection

ⓒ The Author(s) 2022
E. Zouganeli et al. (Eds.): NAIS 2022, CCIS 1650, pp. 52–64, 2022.
https://doi.org/10.1007/978-3-031-17030-0_5

systems, most of the work is still being done by professional journalists in fact checking organizations all around the world[1].

As machine learning is one of the promising techniques for automated fake news detection, one of the obstacles is the amount of accurately labeled training data that are available. Unfortunately, there are very few labeled datasets of sufficient size and quality for supervised learning in this domain. This is due to the scarce resources for manual fact checking and labeling efforts. In addition, because of the new events are introduced continuously, the content and topic of news articles are time-dependent and varied [4]. Weakly supervised learning, a new machine learning paradigm, has been developed to work with low-quality labels called weak labels [19].

In this paper, we present a fake news detection system that uses weakly supervised learning based only on content features. We have chosen to work with full news articles instead of social media posts or shares. Even though the social media is seen as the primary source of the spread of fake news, recent research [27] points out the importance of the coverage of fake news in mainstream media.

Weakly supervised systems can utilize content and contextual features. Previous work using this approach for fake news detection has given promising results [10]. However, the contextual features used in these efforts (e.g. likes, comments, shares) are time-dependent (they change over time), take time to accumulate, and are unavailable for some articles. Therefore, our approach is solely based on the content-based features extracted from the title and content of the articles.

To the best of our knowledge, this is the first work that uses weak supervision for fake news detection by using only content features. Our contributions are three-fold: We introduce a probabilistic weak labeling system that relies only on content features. We collect and present a test dataset from a set of fact-checking organizations including Snopes[2] and PolitiFact[3]. The dataset has been made publicly available on Github[4]. We apply five machine learning classifiers for fake news detection with and without the weak labels to investigate the efficiency of using weak supervised learning with content features.

The rest of the paper is organized as follows: Sect. 2 discusses the state of the art and existing work on weakly supervised methods for fake news detection. Section 3 presents the dataset for the experiments. Section 4 outlines the proposed architecture and experimental design, and presents the findings. Section 5 concludes and gives an outlook to future research directions.

2 Related Work

Even though the fact checking tasks still rely on the professional journalists, the efforts of developing automated fake news detection systems has been in focus of

---

[1] https://reporterslab.org/fact-checking/.
[2] www.snopes.com.
[3] www.politifact.com.
[4] https://github.com/piiingz/fake-news-detection-test-set.

the researchers for the last couple of years. Within these research there is a wide variety of approaches. Crowd-sourcing has been proposed to obtain the labels for fake news [6,17]. However, human annotators can process a limited number of articles. [6] had 90 articles annotated, whereas [17] acquired labels for 240 articles. Crowd sourcing suffers from high costs and doubts in annotations' quality. [35] argues that with a large enough population of fact-checkers, indicating the credibility of articles remains feasible. How to attract and motivate a large enough population remains to be seen. Research on fully automated methods follows different approaches such as content-based, user-based, network-based, and hybrid methods which use the combination of other methods [15]. Content-based methods focus on the analysis of text and non-text content, such as video or sound. For instance, Shrestha et al. [21] combine textual features, sentiment, writing style and psycho-linguistics to identify fake news. User-based methods look at user behaviour and comments to identify fake news [26]. Wang et al. [31] combines a weakly supervised approach with user reports. Network-based methods monitor network activity, which can help to detect bots and investigate the spread patterns. Conversely, Shu et al. [23] reports that humans spread more fake news than bots. In this case, finding out if a user is a real human may help to increase the clues a system collects. Moreover, [23] shows that fake news is more likely to be spread by fake accounts. The computational methods used in the automated detection of fake news is varied. Castelo et al. [4] proposes a topic-agnostic approach to the classification of fake news by using web-markup in addition to LIWC (Linguistic Inquiry and Word Count), and stylistic features. With this approach, they focus on identifying the non-credible web pages spreading fake news instead of detecting individual fake news articles.

Weakly supervised learning (mainly together with contextual features) has been used for fake news detection by many researchers. Helmstetter and Paulheim [10] apply weakly supervised learning to microblogs for detecting fake news in social media and obtain an accuracy of approximately ninety percent. Wang et al. [30] uses reinforcement learning for fake news detection with the use of crowd-sourced labels. Yuan et al. [34] combine weakly supervised learning with a structure-aware multi-head attention network to identify fake news. Weakly supervised learning has been used with content features for tasks such as learning discourse structures in dialogues [2] and building a text classifier in combination with transfer learning [25].

3   Dataset

To choose the best suited dataset for this task, we have reviewed 14 datasets. Table 1 presents an overview of these datasets. Our evaluation considered four properties: size, features, class balance, and labeling method. As a result, we have decided to use the NELA-GT-2019 [9] dataset[5]. The chosen dataset has a large amount of data for all classes. Thus, it supports creating class-balanced subsets. The dataset's features include title and content. The documentation

---

[5] At the time this work started NELA-GT-2020 dataset was unavailable.

of the dataset is excellent. NELA-GT-2019 comprises 1.12M news articles from 260 mainstream and alternative news sources. It has been collected between 01 January 2019 and 31 December 2019. There are four different labels: *reliable, mixed, unreliable,* and *unknown.* In this work, we consider articles labelled *reliable* as credible news and *unreliable* as fake news. We discard the labels *mixed* and *unknown.* The labels in the dataset have been assigned based on the credibility of news sources which does not guarantee the correctness of information itself.

Dataset Collection. For more realistic assessment of the developed models, we have collected an independent dataset which consists of manually fact-checked news articles. So the labels of the news articles in this test set are not based only on the sources they were published on, but on the decision of professional fact checkers. In addition, we payed attention to the publishing date of articles to avoid testing our models on the same news items as were included in the training dataset. Therefore the articles collected for this dataset were published in a different period than NELA-GT-2019. During the collection of this dataset we have used entries from FakeNewsNet[6] [22] and MisInfoText [1] datasets as well as manual collection of articles from Snopes fact-checking archives[7]. The collected dataset includes 434 news articles where half of them is fake and the other half is real news articles. This dataset is available on Github[8].

4   Architecture, Experiments and Results

The proposed system consists of two main components: The weak labeling system and the classification models that use weakly supervised learning. For each of these main components we ran a series of experiments in order to find the best performing models. Then we combine these in our proposed architecture. Figure 1 shows the overall architecture of the proposed system.

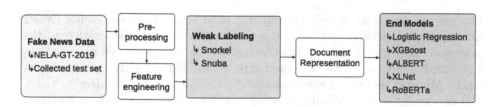

Fig. 1. Overall system architecture

First we apply pre-processing and feature engineering to the raw data. Then the output is passed to the weak labeling system which generates weak

---

[6] https://github.com/KaiDMML/FakeNewsNet.
[7] https://www.snopes.com/fact-check.
[8] https://github.com/piiingz/fake-news-detection-test-set.

Table 1. Fake news datasets reviewed in this work.

Dataset	Type of content	Size
Fakeddit	Reddit posts incl. images, social engagement	1,063,106
FakeNewsCorpus	Articles	9,408,908
FakeNewsNet	Articles, social engagement	1,056
FA-KES	Syrian war articles	804
FEVER	Short statements	185,445
FNID	Statements	15,212
Getting real about fake news	Articles, social engagement	12,999
LIAR	Short statements	12,836
MisInfoText B	Articles	1,380
MisInfoText S	Articles	312
NELA-GT-2018	Articles	713,534
NELA-GT-2019	Articles	1,118,821
NELA-GT-2020	Articles	1,779,127
Twitter	Tweets, user info., social engagement	401,414

labels. After the application of document representation, weakly labelled data is passed to the end model. We have experimented with *Snorkel* and *Snuba*, two weak labeling frameworks, and five classifiers: Logistic Regression, XGBoost [5], ALBERT [12], XLNET [33], and RoBERTa [13].

In the following sections, all these steps are explained in detail and the results from various experiments are presented.

4.1   Data Pre-processing

The pre-processing steps includes applying natural language processing (NLP) techniques such as normalization, stop word removal, and tokenization to the news text. More specifically we have normalized the text, removed punctuation, digits and stop-words, and tokenized into words, bigrams, trigrams and sentences. We used the NLTK word tokenizer[9], NLTK sentence tokenizer[10], NLTK part-of-speech tagger[11], WordNetLemmatizer[12] and Python's built-in lowercasing function. Each step has been applied to both the title and the body of the articles.

---

[9] https://www.nltk.org/api/nltk.tokenize.html#nltk.tokenize.word_tokenize.
[10] https://www.nltk.org/api/nltk.tokenize.html#nltk.tokenize.sent_tokenize.
[11] https://www.nltk.org/_modules/nltk/tag.html#pos_tag.
[12] https://www.nltk.org/_modules/nltk/stem/wordnet.html.

4.2   Feature Engineering

After the pre-processing step, we have determined four types of relevant features based on the literature: stylistic features, complexity features, POS-tagging features, and sentiment features [3,11,16,18].

Stylistic features include author's writing style such as the use of exclamation marks and uppercase words; complexity features include implicit features of the text such as type-token ratio and words per sentence; POS-tagging features include all POS-tag related features such as the presence of verbs, nouns, and adjectives; finally, sentiment features include the sentiment scores of the text such as the scores for subjectivity, positiveness, and negativeness.

In total, we have used 68 extracted features such as *"ratio of stop words"*, *"number of quote marks"*, *"ratio of nouns per word"* and *"document negative score based on sentences"*. A complete list of these features can be found in [8]. For each of these features, the resulting numerical values such as the sentence count, word count etc. are then passed as an input to the weak labeling system.

4.3   Weak Labeling System

The first main component of our architecture focuses on the generation of weak labels for fake news detection. For this, we consider two weak labeling frameworks: Snorkel[13] and Snuba[14]. We have run a set of experiments to compare these two frameworks in the context of fake news detection. Figure 3 shows the overall pipeline of the experiments to evaluate the weak supervised fake news detection.

During our experiments with Snorkel, in order to enhance the performance, we have developed three components for the weak labeling system: *Automatic threshold search, automatic labeling function (LF) generation,* and *labeling function (LF) selection.* In order to create this weak labeling system we have used a small portion of the labeled data we have which is not included in the evaluation of the end models to prevent the data leakage. Figure 2 shows the overall pipeline.

Automatic threshold search takes the instances described with descriptive statistics (such as title word count) as input and selects best feature values (thresholds) that define an instance being fake or real. *Automatic LF generation* component handles the automatic generation of labeling functions in Snorkel. The labels are assigned automatically based on the thresholds defined in the previous step by checking if a feature value of an instance is above or below the threshold. It is also important to find values that cover a large portion of the data set since the higher the coverage the higher the amount of labels assigned is. *LF selection* component handles the possible extremely noisy labels by selecting a portion of LFs. To do that, we evaluated three sets of LFs by using Snorkel's generative model and majority vote approaches: All LFs (*All*), LFs with

---

[13] https://www.snorkel.org.
[14] https://github.com/HazyResearch/reef.

an individual accuracy above 65% ($Acc > 65\%$, this value has been chosen as a result of separate experiments) and top 25 LFs based on their accuracy (*Top 25*).

As a result of our experiments, we have found that the best performing model was Acc > 65% with an accuracy of 0.710 and coverage of 0.860. More details of these components can be found in [8].

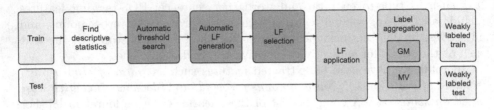

Fig. 2. The pipeline of the automatic weak labeling system in Snorkel. The purple color indicates the components developed in this work. The white color indicates preliminary processing, yellow color indicates the processes handled by Snorkel and the gray color indicates the input and output of the system. (Color figure online)

Snuba framework has been proposed by [29] and it creates heuristics that assign probabilistic labels to instances. Compared to Snorkel, it generates less noisy labels and provides more diversity of instances labeled. In this work we have implemented a weak labeling system using Snuba and tested it with tree types of heuristics, namely decision trees, logistic regression and k-nearest neighbor (KNN). Following the findings of [29] which suggested that the maximum cardinality below four would be sufficient for most real-world tasks, we have experimented with the values below four. Due to the hardware limitations we could not get any results from KNN max cardinality three. The results from these experiments are shown in Table 2. Based on these results we have chosen the best method based on accuracy and coverage. Note that the portion of the data set we have used for these experiments does not contain the data from the weak label generation part to prevent data leakage.

As a result of our experiments with Snorkel and Snuba, we found that Snuba achieves an accuracy of 0.765 and coverage of 0.902, outperforming Snorkel both in terms of accuracy and coverage. We explain this with Snuba's heuristics being more complex than Snorkel and taking the heuristic's diversity into account. Therefore we use Snuba as our weak labeling component. Then, we run the best performing weak labeling system on the *manually labeled test set* to assure that the classifiers would perform better than the weak labeling system so that it is reasonable to train end models. We observed that *Snuba, DT, 3* achieved an accuracy of 0.646, F_1 score of 0.668 and coverage of 0.956.

4.4   Document Representation

Classifiers require the input to come in the form of numerical vectors. We experiment with two different methods to obtain such vectors from the output of

Table 2. The results from the experiments with different types of heuristics of Snuba.

Model	Max cardinality	Accuracy	F1 score	Coverage
DT	1	0.836	0.911	0.077
	2	0.753	0.769	0.873
	3	**0.765**	0.765	0.902
LR	1	0.774	0.845	0.221
	2	0.766	0.816	0.384
	3	0.760	0.777	0.551
k-NN	1	0.610	0.483	1.000
	2	0.650	0.584	1.000
	3	N/A	N/A	N/A

the weak labeling system: TF-IDF and BERT-specific. BERT-based models are designed to deal with raw text which reduces the processing to two simple steps. First, we merge the articles' title and content. Second, we trim the text to conform to the maximum length of token supported by the models. For Logistic regression and XGBoost, we used TF-IDF with an array size of 6000.

4.5 Weakly Supervised Learning

We have trained five models—Logistic Regression, XGBoost, ALBERT, XLNet, and RoBERTa—to determine the best performing classification model for weakly supervised learning in this domain. We have chosen these models based on their previous success for fake news classification [14]. We have also trained the same models as supervised end models for the comparison. Table 3 shows the size of datasets used in this experiment. As it is shown in Fig. 3, both weakly supervised models and supervised models take a portion of the labeled data as input. The weakly supervised models take the weakly labeled data from the weak labeling system as an additional input.

Table 4 presents the results from our experiments with these models using weak labels. Results show that RoBERTa outperforms the four other classifiers, reaching to an accuracy of 0.753, F1 score of 0.779 for supervised and an accuracy of 0.779, F1 score of 0.798 for weakly supervised method on the manually created test set. The second best performing model in this setting is the XLNet with an accuracy of 0.719, F1 score of 0.742 for supervised and an accuracy of 0.733, F1 score of 0.752 for the weakly supervised method. Results of these experiments show that weakly supervised method performs slightly better than the supervised approach. These results also suggest that the combination of weak labeling system and classifier perform better than the weak labeling system alone as it was explained in Sect. 4.3.

In order to understand how the amount of weak labels introduced affects the weakly supervised model, we have experimented with three different ratios of weak labels. Based on the result of the previous experiment, we have used

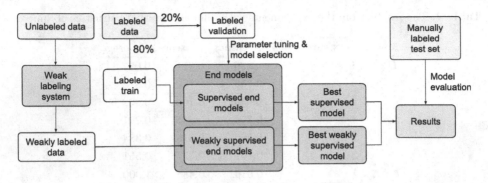

Fig. 3. Experimental pipeline for the end models.

RoBERTa for both weakly supervised and supervised models. First, we have trained our models with all the weak labeled instances (approx. 170K), and then 50K and 25K weak labeled instances respectively, where the total number of instances in the dataset for this set of experiments is approximately 201K. Table 5 shows the results from these experiments. The results of these experiments indicate that the supervised model performs better than the weakly supervised method. As we keep adding more weak labeled data the performance decreases. The weak labeled instances are selected by confidence. This suggests that high-confidence labels contribute best to the detection, whereas low-confidence labels spoil the performance. However, results also show that the difference between these models, (especially the supervised, weak 25K and weak 50K) is marginal. Given that we have tested our system with only one test set, we do not know how the results would change for other datasets. Additionally, our test set is relatively small compared to the training set (see Table 3). We expect weakly supervised models to perform better in conditions where the test set is similar or larger in size as the training data set. We believe that weakly supervised learning for fake news detection is a promising method and should be explored further. Also more research is required to verify the effect of weakly labeled data for fake news detection.

Table 3. Size of datasets used.

	# of samples	Origin dataset
Labeled training set	1 380	NELA-19
Unlabeled training set	201 604	NELA-19
Weakly labeled training set	5 520	NELA-19
Labeled validation set	345	NELA-19
Manually labeled test set	434	Manual

Table 4. Comparison of classifiers. For each of the five classifiers, we list the scores on the *manually created test set*, as well as the difference between the usage of weakly supervised labels. The rows refer to Logistic Regression (LR), XGBoost (XG), ALBERT (AL), XLNet (XL), and RoBERTa (Ro).

	Accuracy			F_1		
	Supervised	Weak	Δ	Supervised	Weak	Δ
LR	0.624	0.641	−0.017	0.630	0.653	−0.023
XG	0.578	0.618	−0.040	0.592	0.623	−0.031
AL	0.696	0.696	0.000	0.726	0.717	0.009
XL	0.719	0.733	−0.014	0.742	0.752	−0.010
Ro	**0.753**	**0.779**	−0.026	**0.779**	**0.798**	−0.019

Table 5. The comparison of supervised and weakly supervised models with different ratios of weak labels.

	Validation		Test set	
	Accuracy	F1 score	Accuracy	F1 score
$Weak_{all}$	0.800	0.808	0.671	0.721
$Weak_{50k}$	0.900	0.901	0.753	0.778
$Weak_{25k}$	0.942	0.942	0.781	0.801
Supervised	**0.959**	**0.959**	**0.793**	**0.813**

5   Conclusions and Future Work

Automation will remain necessary to combat fake news as long as fact-checkers remain a scarce resource. Fake news classifiers rely on accurate labels. This work proposed and explored the use of weakly supervised learning that relies only on the content features. Our observations on the performance of different weak labeling frameworks suggest that Snuba performs better than Snorkel for this task. As a result of our experiments with five different classifiers, RoBERTa outperformed the other four classifiers both in supervised and weakly supervised tasks. We tested the weak labels' utility for fake news detection with help of the NELA-GT-2019 data set and a manually created test set where it has been made publicly available. We observed that the more weak labels we introduced, the more the classification performance dropped. However, this decrease is not significant. Therefore weakly supervised learning may be a suitable method to use in the absence of labeled data. More research is necessary to investigate successful ways to blend weak labels without compromising performance.

As a future work, we intend to use additional data sets to verify our findings. Further, we will explore how to effectively use confidence score to estimate weak label's effect.

References

1. Asr, F.T., Taboada, M.: MisInfoText. A collection of news articles, with false and true labels (2019). https://github.com/sfu-discourse-lab/Misinformation_detection
2. Badene, S., Thompson, K., Lorré, J., Asher, N.: Weak supervision for learning discourse structure. In: EMNLP/IJCNLP (2019)
3. Bhutani, B., Rastogi, N., Sehgal, P., Purwar, A.: Fake news detection using sentiment analysis. In: 2019 12th International Conference on Contemporary Computing, IC3 2019 (2019). https://doi.org/10.1109/IC3.2019.8844880
4. Castelo, S., et al.: A topic-agnostic approach for identifying fake news pages. In: Companion Proceedings of the 2019 World Wide Web Conference (2019)
5. Chen, T., et al.: XGBoost: extreme gradient boosting. R package version 0.4-2 1(4), 1–4 (2015)
6. Färber, M., Burkard, V., Jatowt, A., Lim, S.: A multidimensional dataset based on crowdsourcing for analyzing and detecting news bias. In: Proceedings of the 29th ACM International Conference on Information & Knowledge Management, pp. 3007–3014 (2020)
7. Fernández-Torres, M.J., Almansa-Martínez, A., Chamizo-Sánchez, R.: Infodemic and fake news in Spain during the COVID-19 pandemic. Int. J. Environ. Res. Public Health 18(4), 1781 (2021)
8. From, A.R., Netland, I.U.: Fake news detection by weakly supervised learning: a content-based approach. Master's thesis, NTNU (2021)
9. Gruppi, M., Horne, B.D., Adalı, S.: NELA-GT-2019: a large multi-labelled news dataset for the study of misinformation in news articles (2020)
10. Helmstetter, S., Paulheim, H.: Weakly supervised learning for fake news detection on Twitter. In: 2018 IEEE/ACM International Conference on Advances in Social Networks Analysis and Mining (ASONAM), pp. 274–277. IEEE (2018)
11. Horne, B.D., Adali, S.: This just in: fake news packs a lot in title, uses simpler, repetitive content in text body, more similar to satire than real news. In: Proceedings of the First Workshop on Fact Extraction and Verification, pp. 40–49, March 2017. http://arxiv.org/abs/1703.09398
12. Lan, Z., Chen, M., Goodman, S., Gimpel, K., Sharma, P., Soricut, R.: ALBERT: a lite BERT for self-supervised learning of language representations. arXiv preprint arXiv:1909.11942 (2019)
13. Liu, Y., et al.: RoBERTa: a robustly optimized BERT pretraining approach (2019)
14. Oshikawa, R., Qian, J., Wang, W.Y.: A survey on natural language processing for fake news detection. In: Proceedings of the 12th Language Resources and Evaluation Conference, Marseille, France, pp. 6086–6093. European Language Resources Association, May 2020. https://aclanthology.org/2020.lrec-1.747
15. Özgöbek, Ö., Gulla, J.A.: Towards an understanding of fake news. In: CEUR Workshop Proceedings, vol. 2041, pp. 35–42 (2017)
16. Pennebaker, J.W., Francis, M.E., Booth, R.J.: Linguistic Inquiry and Word Count. Lawrence Erlbaum Associates (2001)
17. Pérez-Rosas, V., Kleinberg, B., Lefevre, A., Mihalcea, R.: Automatic detection of fake news. arXiv preprint arXiv:1708.07104 (2017)
18. Rashkin, H., Choi, E., Jang, J.Y., Volkova, S., Choi, Y.: Truth of varying shades: analyzing language in fake news and political fact-checking. In: Proceedings of the 2017 Conference on Empirical Methods in Natural Language Processing, Stroudsburg, PA, USA, pp. 2931–2937. Association for Computational Linguistics (2017). https://doi.org/10.18653/v1/D17-1317. http://aclweb.org/anthology/D17-1317

19. Ratner, A., Varma, P., Hancock, B., Ré, C.: Weak supervision: the new programming paradigm for machine learning (2017). http://ai.stanford.edu/blog/weak-supervision/

20. Rodrigues, U.M., Xu, J.: Regulation of COVID-19 fake news infodemic in China and India. Media Int. Aust. **177**(1), 125–131 (2020)

21. Shrestha, A., Spezzano, F., Joy, A.: Detecting fake news spreaders in social networks via linguistic and personality features. In: CLEF (2020)

22. Shu, K., Mahudeswaran, D., Wang, S., Lee, D., Liu, H.: FakeNewsNet: a data repository with news content, social context and spatialtemporal information for studying fake news on social media (2019)

23. Shu, K., Wang, S., Liu, H.: Understanding user profiles on social media for fake news detection (2018). https://doi.org/10.1109/MIPR.2018.00092

24. Spohr, D.: Fake news and ideological polarization: filter bubbles and selective exposure on social media. Bus. Inf. Rev. **34**(3), 150–160 (2017). https://doi.org/10.1177/0266382117722446

25. Starosta, A.: Building NLP classifiers cheaply with transfer learning and weak supervision (2019). https://web.stanford.edu/class/archive/cs/cs224n/cs224n.1194/reports/custom/15577251.pdf

26. Tacchini, E., Ballarin, G., Della Vedova, M.L., Moret, S., de Alfaro, L.: Some like it hoax: automated fake news detection in social networks. arXiv preprint arXiv:1704.07506 (2017)

27. Tsfati, Y., Boomgaarden, H.G., Strömbäck, J., Vliegenthart, R., Damstra, A., Lindgren, E.: Causes and consequences of mainstream media dissemination of fake news: literature review and synthesis. Ann. Int. Commun. Assoc. **44**(2), 157–173 (2020)

28. Van Der Linden, S., Panagopoulos, C., Roozenbeek, J.: You are fake news: political bias in perceptions of fake news. Media Cult. Soc. **42**(3), 460–470 (2020)

29. Varma, P., Ré, C.: Snuba. Proc. VLDB Endow. **12**(3), 223–236 (2018). https://doi.org/10.14778/3291264.3291268

30. Wang, Y., et al.: Weak supervision for fake news detection via reinforcement learning, December 2019. http://arxiv.org/abs/1912.12520

31. Wang, Y., et al.: Weak supervision for fake news detection via reinforcement learning. In: Proceedings of the AAAI Conference on Artificial Intelligence, vol. 34, pp. 516–523 (2020)

32. Wendling, M.: The (almost) complete history of 'fake news', January 2018

33. Yang, Z., Dai, Z., Yang, Y., Carbonell, J., Salakhutdinov, R.R., Le, Q.V.: XLNet: generalized autoregressive pretraining for language understanding. In: Advances in Neural Information Processing Systems, vol. 32 (2019)

34. Yuan, C., Ma, Q., Zhou, W., Han, J., Hu, S.: Early detection of fake news by utilizing the credibility of news, publishers, and users based on weakly supervised learning. In: Proceedings of the 28th International Conference on Computational Linguistics, Barcelona, Spain, pp. 5444–5454. International Committee on Computational Linguistics, December 2020. https://doi.org/10.18653/v1/2020.coling-main.475. https://aclanthology.org/2020.coling-main.475

35. Zhou, X., Zafarani, R.: A survey of fake news. ACM Comput. Surv. **53**(5), 1–40 (2020). https://doi.org/10.1145/3395046

Improving the Usability of Tabular Data Through Data Annotation, Repair and Augmentation

Rabeb Abida[(⊠)] and Anthony Cleve

PReCISE, NaDI, Faculty of Computer Science, University of Namur, Namur, Belgium
{rabeb.abida,anthony.cleve}@unamur.be

Abstract. In recent years, a rapidly increasing amount of information has been made publicly available in tabular form on the Web. Many of these data are not usable due to their poor quality (e.g., misspelled or missing values, missing or incomplete metadata, and missing meaningful columns). Solutions have been proposed in the literature to address these data quality issues, but there is still a lack of all-in-one approaches that can fully solve them. Therefore, users need to use several methods to solve these data quality issues. In this paper, we present an all-in-one and automatic approach called SINATRA that helps to bridge this gaps by providing the following features: *data annotation* (to address misspelled and incomplete metadata issues), *data repair* (to address missing values (data) issues), and *data augmentation* (to dynamically add meaningful columns and corresponding cell values to the dataset). An evaluation of the SINATRA approach based on datasets from a state-of-the-art benchmark shows promising results in terms of F1-measure and precision.

Keywords: Usability · Tabular data · Data annotation · Data repairing · Data augmentation

1 Introduction

Nowadays a vast amount of information is provided on the Web in unstructured text, semi-structured data, and more structured data in the form of tables [2,4, 10,12]. They can sometimes be difficult to use due to data quality issues, such as misspellings and missing metadata, ambiguity in table cells, missing cell values, and missing significant columns [4,6–8,10,12].

Several methods have been proposed in the literature to solve the aforementioned issues. On the one hand, the use of *Semantic Table Annotation* (STA), also known as *data annotation*, consists of assigning semantic tags from knowledge graphs (KGs) (e.g., Wikidata [15] and DBpedia [3]) to the data columns elements. The *data annotation* has proven to effectively solve the problem of spelling errors and missing or incomplete metadata [8–10,12,13]. On the other hand, *data repair* handles the problem of missing cell data (values), and *data augmentation* adds meaningful columns and corresponding cell values to the

© The Author(s) 2022
E. Zouganeli et al. (Eds.): NAIS 2022, CCIS 1650, pp. 65–77, 2022.
https://doi.org/10.1007/978-3-031-17030-0_6

data. As part of the "Tabular Data to knowledge Graph Matching" competition [9], some approaches have implemented the STA process, such as [8,10,12], but they have not incorporated *data repair* and *augmentation* phases. Meanwhile, other works such as OpenRefine[1] and Magic [13] propose a system that is capable of both annotating and augmenting a dataset, but they do not support any *data repair* phase.

Despite the systems proposed in the literature to solve these data quality issues, there is still no all-in-one approach that can handle them, and nor are there other features that can further support the STA process. Therefore, users need to use multiple methods to tackle these problems.

In this paper, we present an all-in-one and fully automatic proposal called SINATRA (**S**emant**I**c a**N**notation **A**ugmenta**T**ion and **R**ep**A**ir) that helps fill these gaps by providing the following features:

(i) ***data annotation*** is used to resolve spelling errors and missing or incomplete metadata. It is based on the STA process, which consists of three main tasks: Column type Annotation (CTA) (Fig. 1c), Column property annotation (CPA) (Fig. 1a) and Column Entity Annotation (CEA) (Fig. 1b). They assigned the data elements to the concepts in the knowledge graph (DBpedia KG), as shown in Fig. 1. To describe each task in the STA process [12], we consider a table of real dataset[2] in Fig. 1, which presents the names of the presidents (col1) and their place of birth (col2).

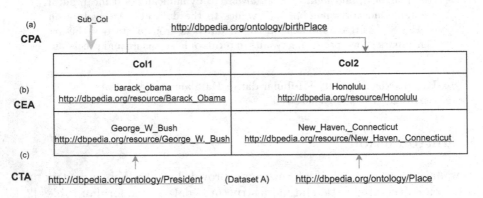

Fig. 1. Data annotation. Tabular data (black) is annotated with the properties (magenta), entities (blue), and types (green) from DBpedia as asked in the CPA (a), CEA (b), and CTA (c) tasks respectively. (Color figure online)

(ii) ***data repair*** is used to handle missing or incomplete cell values in the dataset. It is based on a method that applies SPARQL queries to fetch missing cell values from the DBpedia KG. Figure 2 shows an example of the data repair phase by adding a cell value "http://dbpedia.org/resource/Honolulu".

---

[1] https://openrefine.org/.

[2] https://tinyurl.com/4hrx6s48.

(iii) **data augmentation** is used to dynamically add meaningful columns and their corresponding cell values to the dataset. It is based on a method that applies (i) SPARQL queries to fetch the property URIs (CPA) of the new columns proposed by users and (ii) SPARQL queries to fulfill the corresponding cell values of the newly added columns. Figure 2 shows an example the data augmentation feature by adding a new column "http://dbpedia.org/ontology/birthDate".

http://dbpedia.org/ontology/President	http://dbpedia.org/ontology/birthPlace	
http://dbpedia.org/resource/Barack_Obama		
http://dbpedia.org/resource/George_W._Bush	http://dbpedia.org/resource/New_Haven,_Connecticut	

http://dbpedia.org/ontology/President	http://dbpedia.org/ontology/birthPlace	http://dbpedia.org/ontology/birthDate
http://dbpedia.org/resource/Barack_Obama	http://dbpedia.org/resource/Honolulu	1961-08-04
http://dbpedia.org/resource/George_W._Bush	http://dbpedia.org/resource/New_Haven,_Connecticut	1946-07-06

Fig. 2. Example of *data repair* by adding cell value "http://dbpedia.org/resource/Honolulu" (light green) and *data augmentation* by adding new column "http://dbpedia.org/ontology/birthDate" (light blue). (Color figure online)

For evaluating our approach, we used some of the datasets proposed by the "Tabular Data to knowledge Graph Matching" [9,10] competition to measure the effectiveness of the SINATRA approach by F1-measure and precision metrics and demonstrate the capability of its features.

The remainder of the paper is organized as follows. Section 2 positions our work with respect to related literature. Section 3 gives an overview of our approach, describes in detail the different phases it covers, and presents its implementation. Section 4 evaluates SINATRA and assesses the effectiveness of its phases. Section 5 concludes this paper and anticipates future research directions.

2   Related Work

This section reviews related work on popular approaches and tools that address gaps in data quality issues (e.g., misspelled or missing values, missing or incomplete metadata, and missing meaningful columns). We present them with their respective features, strengths and weaknesses.

Some works have been proposed, mainly with a particular and non-integrated focus on data pre-processing, subject column (Sub_Col) detection [13]. Furthermore, OpenRefine and [11,14] rely only on their own data (domain-independent) and perform only a few steps of the STI process. They can be classified as supervised (Sup: they exploit already annotated tables for training) and semi-automatic. Other works [8,10,12,13] can be classified as unsupervised (Unsp:

they do not require training data) and automatic. They do not provide a user-friendly graphical interface, and manually annotating the data is time-consuming for the user.

The STA process [10] is composed of five steps which are: (i) the data pre-processing, which aims to prepare the data inside the table; (ii) the detection of the Sub_Col is designed to detect the main column of the table; and (iii) the three sub-steps for the *data annotation*, which are CEA task (Fig. 1b), CTA task (Fig. 1c), and CPA task (Fig. 1a). Other proposals have been made to resolve the gaps in the above-mentioned approaches and perform all the steps of the STA process. In this way, [8,10,12] propose novel techniques to improve and provide high-quality annotations to address the issues of misspelling and missing or incomplete metadata. They used unsupervised learning techniques, which could be applied to general-purpose domains, and utilized Open Source KG that was freely available on the Web (DBpedia). MantisTable [8] used some features to resolve the limitation of the Subject Column (Sub_Col) task. It allowed users to apply a series of steps to prepare data and used different features to automatically assign the Sub_Col. MTab [12] tool as an automatic semantic annotation system, could jointly deal with the three tasks CTA, CEA and CPA. It was based on the joint probability distribution of multiple tables to DBpedia KG matching. MTab achieved impressive empirical performance for the three annotation tasks of the STA process and won the first prize at the SemTab challenge [9,10]. MTab did not offer subject column detection but has excellent results and MantisTable did not offer excellent results like MTab but allowed Sub_Col detection [9,10]. Those systems [8,10–12,14] can not create or add new columns to *augment* the annotation with additional knowledge graph (KG).

However, OpenRefine and Magic [13] have offered systems capable of both annotating and augmenting a dataset. OpenRefine can perform a semi-automatic reconciliation process against any database that exposes a Web service using Reconciliation Service API[3] specification or a SPARQL endpoint. This tool requires the user to manually correct a cell that has multiple entities (CEA). In addition, it is also able to create new columns through facets, where the user has to formulate the URL to fetch the URIs. Magic [13] offered a system capable of annotating a dataset using the interpretable embedding technique and utilized KGs (DBpedia, WikiData). It can be added a column to further *augment* the Tabular Data. It did not do the pre-processing data phase and used techniques, which were already proposed by the state-of-the-art approaches for that particular phase. Magic might not be outperform the existing state-of-the-art techniques to generate such annotations [1]. Despite all their achievements and results, these proposed tools are not in a position to solve the problems of missing cell values. They do not include the *data repair* phase.

In addition, in the R&D community, there is a lack of automated support [2,5], which can combine the appropriate features defined in Table 1 to assist users in overcoming data quality issues.

---

[3] https://github.com/OpenRefine/OpenRefine/wiki/Reconciliation-Service-API.

Table 1 summarizes the selected approaches and tools that meet certain features: *Data annotation, Data repair* and *Data augmentation*, and shows the difference between them and our proposed approach SINATRA.

Table 1. Approaches and tools that support the above features: *Data annotation, Data repair* and *Data augmentation*.

Approach & tools	STA process (data annotation feature)						Features		KGs/ontology import	Export
	Learning techniques	Data pre-pro	Sub-col	CEA	CTA	CPA	Data aug. (add-col)	Data repair (add missing cell values)		
Open refine	Sup	x	-	x	-	x	x	x/-	Wikidata FreeBase	x
Odalic [11]	Sup	-	-	x	-	x	-	-	DBpedia Dom.Ind	x
DataGraft [14]	Sup	-	-	x	x	-	-	-	Dom.Ind	-
MantisTable [8]	Unsup	x	x	x	x	x	-	-	DBpedia	-
MTab [12]	Unsup	x	x	x	x	x	-	-	DBpedia	-
Magic [13]	Unsup	-	x	x	x	x	x	-	WikiData	-
SINATRA	Unsup	x	x	x	x	x	x	x	DBpedia	x

SINATRA is a solution designed as an all-in-one and automatic approach based on MantisTable [8] and MTab [12] systems, which will be described in Sect. 3.

3   The SINATRA Approach

This section describes a fully automatic approach, which combines all methods and tools into one integrated approach.

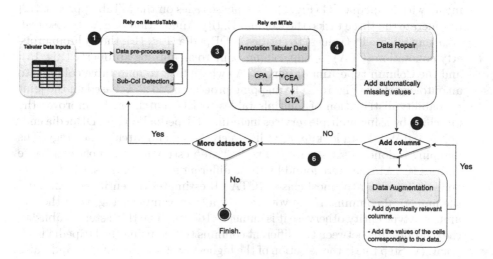

Fig. 3. An overview of **SINATRA** approach (tool).

This proposal overcomes the associated difficulties with data quality on the Web, especially tabular data. More details on the implementation of the approach are available online[4]. It implements its features: *Data annotation, Data repair* and *Data augmentation* through the following four phases such as, **Data pre-processing** and **Subject Column (Sub_Col) detection, Data Annotation, Data repair**, and **Data augmentation**, which Fig. 3 presents an overview of the proposal.

1. During the **Data pre-processing and Sub_Col detection** phase, the SINATRA approach takes as input a large number of local Excel or CSV datasets on the user's computer in order to focus the users to automatically prepare the datasets and detect the Sub-Col before applying the data annotation phase. This phase is based on the Mantistable approach [8] and consists of two steps: (i) Data pre-processing step, the process begins to clean and uniform Data inside the table, remove HTML tags, stop words and some character (i.e.," '), turn text into lowercase, delete of text in brackets, and normalize measurements units. Once this step is complete, the system switches to detect (ii) the Sub_Col. It is as the Subject of relationships among columns, and the annotation of other columns as Objects (Fig. 1 represented Sub_Col by the orange color). This step starts by determining the literal columns (e.g., address, phone number, URL, color) using regular expressions. Once this step is complete, the system chooses from remaining columns (called Named Entity columns), the subject column (Sub_Col) based on different statistic features, such as the average number of words in each cell, fraction of empty cells in the column, the fraction of cells with unique content, and distance from the first-named entity column [8]. More details on those steps can be found in [8]. Once the phase has finished, it moves on to the second phase, which consists of annotating the dataset.

2. Data Annotation phase aims to automatically annotate Tabular data elements with DBpedia KG (Fig. 1). This phase relies on the MTab approach [12] to generate the three tasks: the Column Entity Annotation (CEA), whose task is to map table cells (values) to entities in DBpedia (Fig. 1b); the Column property annotation (CPA) to map column-pairs to an ontology property (Fig. 1a); and the Column type Annotation (CTA) whose task to map table columns to an ontology class (Fig. 1c). The mapping process in MTab is based on the joint probability distribution of multiple tables to KG matching. It improves the matching by using multiple services including, DBpedia Lookup, DBpedia endpoint, and WikiData lookup, as well as a cross-lingual matching strategy. Ths mapping is done in six steps. (i) The first step estimates the most candidate entities (CEA) that were found by those different search services. (ii) The second step is to infer the most classes (CTA). It estimates the entity columns and the numerical columns. If the vote returns a text or integer tag, then the column is of type entity otherwise it is numeric [16]. (iii) The third step establishes the relationships between the different columns (CPA) using the DBpedia Endpoint. (v) Step five is the selection of the highest probabilities of the candidates

---

[4] https://github.com/123rabida123/SINATRA-Annotation-Repair-Augmentation.

(CEA) in step four to establish their relationship (CPA) via a majority vote. (vi) Step six corresponds to the selection of the highest probabilities of the candidates (CEA) in step four to establish their type (CTA) via the majority vote. More details about each step of MTab can be found in [12]. Our contribution in the first two phases is that combined the strengths of MantisTable and MTab to perform both sub-steps.

MTab does not offer a Sub_Col detection phase but has excellent results in annotating data solves misspelling issues; and MantisTable does not offer excellent results like MTab but allows Sub_Col detection.

Once the data annotation phase completes, we get an annotated dataset, but some cells in this dataset still have null values "nan" (Fig. 4a). Hence, we can observe the MTab system's shortcoming, which cannot add the missing cell values in the datasets, as shown in the example in the screenshots (Fig. 4a).

3. Data repair phase aims to automatically add missing cell entities (values) or undefined values "nan". Our algorithm applies SPARQL queries by taking the cell entity (CEA) of the Sub_Col and the column property (CPA) (e.g., CEA + CPA) to retrieve the missing cell entities (CEA). An example of a SPARQL query to get the missing cell entity of the first row in the above dataset (Fig. 2).

In some cases, the query returns ambiguous entities. In this case, our algorithm calculates the pre-score of each entity using the *confidence-score* (CFS) of the Sub_Col entity and the cell entity, and determines the relationship. If there is a relation (CPA) between them (Sub_Col entity and Cell entity), the CFS increases by 1. For example, CFS (honolulu) = 1, CFS (Honolulu) = 1 and there is a relation between "barack_Obama" and "Honolulu", hence CFS = 2. The SPARQL query (Listing 1.1) retrieves an object for the content of the column "http://dbpedia.org/ontology/birthPlace" (Property/Predicate) and the subject of the first row "http://dbpedia.org/resource/barack_Obama" from DBpedia KG, where the cell entity (object) retrieved by the query (Listing 1.1) is "http://dbpedia.org/resource/Honolulu" (Fig. 4b).

```
{
PREFIX dbr: <http://dbpedia.org/resource/>
    SELECT ?object
    WHERE
        { <http://dbpedia.org/resource/barack_Obama>
          <http://dbpedia.org/ontology/birthPlace>
          ?object
        }
}
```

Listing 1.1. SPARQL query to retrieve a cell entity (Object).

4. During the **Data augmentation** phase, the system allows the user to add relevant columns to the annotated dataset (Fig. 2). The user simply enters a word "new-Column" (Listing 1.2) to choose a CPA (URI of the new column) in the proposal list of this approach. For the same word (e.g., new-Column = "birth"), there can be several URIs (CPA) that appear in this list, such as: "http://dbpedia.org/ontology/birthDate" and "http://dbpedia.org/ontology/birthDeath". The user chooses the one CPA, and SINATRA will be added as a new column to the dataset, or she/he can enter the name of the column exactly as "birthDate". Therefore, the system allows the user to add the chosen CPA "http://dbpedia.org/ontology/birthDate" if it is not already in this annotated dataset (Fig. 4c). The algorithm has created a list of CPA proposals, where, each time the query (Listing 1.2) returns a CPA (Predicate has an rdf:property), which contains a word proposed by the user, it stores it in this list.

```
{
PREFIX dbr: <http://dbpedia.org/resource/>
    SELECT ?predicate
    WHERE {
            ?predicate a rdf:Property
            FILTER ( REGEX ( STR (?predicate), http://dbpedia.org/ontology/, i) )
            FILTER ( REGEX ( STR (?predicate), "_+_new-Column_+_", i ) )
    }
ORDER BY ?predicate
}
```

Listing 1.2. Generic query to detect predicates from a SPARQL endpoint to add column.

Once the user chooses a CPA, the system creates a new empty column and then applies the same SPARQL queries (Listing 1.1) of the *data repair* phase to fulfill the corresponding cell entities of the newly added column.

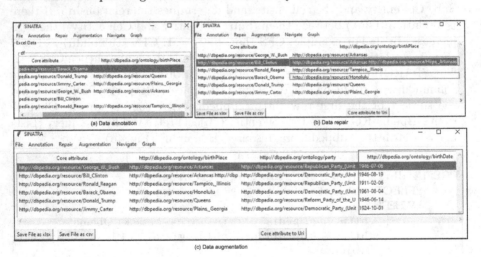

(a) Data annotation

(b) Data repair

(c) Data augmentation

Fig. 4. Screenshots of the *data annotation*(a), *data repair*(b), and *data augmentation*(c) features of SINATRA.

According to the user's request, the data augmentation phase can create more than one column, as illustrated in step 5 of the (Fig. 3). When the system has finished the previous phases, if there are still datasets to annotate, it restarts the first phase and executes the same phases of the SINATRA process (Fig. 3). SINATRA saves the annotated datasets in a local folder and can be exported in Excel (XLSX) and CSV format.

Figure 4 depicts the graphical interface of SINATRA and focuses on data annotation (a), data repair (b), and data augmentation (c) features. We chose to use the python library *Tkinter*[5] to develop the graphical interface. Visually, tkinter is less pretty than other extensions, but it is better to check the frequency of updates of their source code before choosing one, and its license is more flexible. The implementation of the SINATRA approach, which source code is available on GitHub[6] for future research.

4   Evaluation and Demonstration

This section presents the detail about benchmark datasets, ground truths, and evaluation metrics in Sect. 4.1, followed by the evaluation results and demonstration in Sect. 4.2. This evaluation aims to measure the performance of the *data repair* and *data augmentation* features of the SINATRA approach. In the next section, we present the results of the evaluation and the demonstration of its features.

4.1   Datasets, Ground Truths and Measures

To evaluate this proposal using randomized datasets[7] and the ground truths proposed by the SemTab competition [9,10]. These ground truths are composed of three targets (CEA-targets, CPA-targets, and CTA-targets)[8] matching with DBpedia KG for each annotation task (CEA, CTA, and CPA).

In Table 2, we present the datasets used in our evaluation: Reference of the Dataset, Dataset, #Col, #Rows, and Names of columns.

Table 2. The characteristics of the datasets were evaluated by SINATRA approach

Ref	Datasets	#Col	#Rows	Name of columns
D1	211	4	56	Col1: University of UEA; Col2: President; Col3: number of staff; Col4: Surface area
D2	212	4	15	Col1: University; Col2: Post holde; Col3: Number of students; Col4: Number of staff
D3	274	5	17	Col1: Name of the animal; Col2: Family of the animal; Col3: (unnamed); Col4: Location; Col5: (unnamed)
D4	275	5	65	Col1: Name of the animal; Col2: Family of the animal; Col3: Place; Col4: (unnamed); Col5: (unnamed)
D5	308	4	78	Col1: Group event; Col2: County; Col3: Company; Col4: (unnamed)
D6	309	6	44	Col1: Group event; Col2: Second team; Col3: Third team; Col4: Second driver country; Col5: Third driver country; Col6: (unnamed)

---

[5] https://docs.python.org/fr/3/library/tkinter.html.

[6] https://github.com/123rabida123/SINATRA-Annotation-Repair-Augmentation.

[7] https://zenodo.org/record/3518539#.YoOgK6hBwuU.

[8] https://www.aicrowd.com/challenges/semtab-2020.

To measure the efficiency of the *data repair* and *data augmentation* features of the SINATRA process, we used the following metrics proposed in [9,10]: Precision (P), Recall (R), and F-measure(F1).

(P), (R) and (F1) of the mapping between the datasets and the DBpedia KG are calculated using the following formula: where a *perfect annotation* refers to the annotation returned by our approach, which corresponds to the annotations of ground truths, a *submitted annotation* refers to the annotation returned by our approach and a *ground truth annotations* corresponds to the number of annotations in the Target Tables. We combined the predefined measures, which represent the harmonic mean between P and R to calculate F1.

$$P = \frac{(\#perfect\ annotations)}{(\#submitted\ annotations)}\ (1)\ R = \frac{(\#perfect\ annotations)}{(\#ground\ truth\ annotations)}(2)\ F1 = \frac{(2*P*R)}{(P+R)}(3)$$

4.2   Evaluation Results and Demonstration

This section evaluates and demonstrates the performance of the SINATRA approach's features. For more details on the results of the evaluation, consulting our Github[9].

Regarding the evaluation of the **data annotation** feature, this phase of SINATRA is based on the MTab approach. Therefore, it automatically has the same performance as MTab. Table 3 below shows the results of the evaluation of the *data annotation* phase by the MTab approach [12].

Table 3. Evaluation results of the *data annotation* feature by MTab approach.

Feature	Data annotation (MTab approach)					
Tasks / Datasets	CEA		CPA		CTA	
Measures	F1	P	F1	P	F1	P
D1	1.0	1.0	0.881	0.929	0.850	0.852
D2	1.0	1.0	0.877	0.929	0.850	0.850
D3	0.983	0.983	0.844	0.845	0.833	0.833
D4	0.970	0.970	0.832	0.832	0.825	0.825
D5	1.0	1.0	0.987	0.975	0.929	0.933
D6	1.0	1.0	0.965	0.991	0.970	0.970

Our goal in this evaluation is to compare the results of the *data repair* and *data augmentation* phases (Table 4) with the results of the *data annotation* phase (Table 3) to show that they can correctly add the data (entities) and the missing columns.

Regarding the evaluation of the **data repair** feature, we re-based on the same datasets as above (Table 2). In this phase, the evaluation is based on two factors: The first factor (1): we removed some values from those datasets (Table 2) and calculated the performance of this phase. The second factor (2): we added the missing cell values into these datasets during the *data repair* phase. Table 4 below

---

[9] https://github.com/123rabida123/Datasets-and-Results-of-evaluation-SDA.

shows the performance results of the data repair phase based on the two factors mentioned. From the results of Table 4, we notice the results of the CEA task are reduced in the factor (1) because (R) is reduced (the removed URIs (entities) are in the CEA-targets). Based on the factor (2), we highlight that this phase can add missing data very nicely, where the CEA task has $F1 = 1$ of the datasets (D1 and D2). They have the same results as the *data annotation* feature. The CEA results are represented by the yellow color in Table 4. For the datasets (D5 and D6), the results of the CEA task have been reduced a little bit (from $F1 = 1$ in Data annotation to $F1 = 0.987$ in Data repair), because some URIs were not perfect or were not available in the CEA-targets. The CPA task is represented by magenta color and the CTA task is represented by cyan color, which have no variation in both factors. They have the same results as the *data annotation* feature in Table 3.

Table 4. Evaluation results of the *data repair* and *data augmentation* features.

Feature	Data repair											
Factors	Remove cell values (1)						Add missing cell values (2)					
Tasks	CEA		CPA		CTA		CEA		CPA		CTA	
Measures/ Datasets	F1	P	F1	P	F1	P	F1	P	F1	P	F1	P
D1	0.854	0.845	0.881	0.929	0.850	0.852	1.0	1.0	0.881	0.929	0.850	0.852
D2	0.852	0.874	0.877	0.929	0.850	0.850	1.0	1.0	0.877	0.929	0.850	0.852
D3	0.832	0.832	0.844	0.845	0.833	0.833	0.877	0.877	0.844	0.845	0.833	0.833
D4	0.812	0.813	0.832	0.832	0.825	0.825	0.834	0.836	0.832	0.832	0.825	0.825
D5	0.911	0.911	0.987	0.975	0.929	0.933	0.983	0.983	0.987	0.975	0.929	0.933
D6	0.943	0.945	0.965	0.991	0.970	0.970	0.987	0.975	0.965	0.991	0.970	0.970
Feature	Data augmentation											
Factors	Remove Column (1)						Add missing Column (2)					
Tasks	CEA		CPA		CTA		CEA		CPA		CTA	
Measures/ Datasets	F1	P	F1	P	F1	P	F1	P	F1	P	F1	P
D1	0.750	0.753	0.706	0.738	0.754	0.70	1.0	1.0	0.881	0.929	0.850	0.852
D2	0.751	0.754	0.706	0.738	0.736	0.739	1.0	1.0	0.881	0.929	0.850	0.852
D3	0.606	0.638	0.754	0.700	0.729	0.781	0.981	0.981	0.844	0.845	0.833	0.833
D4	0.632	0.634	0.707	0.717	0.729	0.781	0.943	0.945	0.844	0.845	0.833	0.833
D5	0.913	0.915	0.846	0.855	0.860	0.878	1.0	1.0	0.987	0.975	0.929	0.934
D6	0.845	0.845	0.846	0.855	0.833	0.835	0.996	0.997	0.939	0.987	0.956	0.956

Regarding the evaluation of the **data augmentation** feature, we re-used the same datasets as above (Table 2). The evaluation of the data augmentation feature is based on two factors: In the first factor (1), we removed every second column from those datasets (Table 2) and calculated the performance of this phase (without the second columns). In the second factor (2), we added the missing columns into these datasets. Table 4 above shows the performance results of this phase based on the two factors mentioned: whether this proposal is able to add exactly the deleted column in each dataset. From the results of the factor (1) in Table 4, we notice that the results of the CEA, CPA, and CTA tasks are more reduced because (R) is reduced (the removed URIs (entities) are in the targets). In addition, we notice from the results of the factor (2) in Table 4, that this feature is able to add the missing column very well, where the CEA, CPA, and CTA tasks of the datasets (D1, D2, and D5) have the same results as the *data annotation* feature in Table 3 are represented by the yellow color. The magenta color represents the results of the CPA task, and the CTA task is represented by the cyan color of the datasets (D1, D2, D3, D4, and D5). They also have the same results as the *data annotation* feature. Thus, the *data augmentation* feature is perfectly able to add missing columns to the datasets. For the datasets (D3, D4, and D6), the results of the CEA task were slightly reduced, because some URIs were not perfect or were not available in the CEA targets.

5   Conclusion and Future Work

In this paper, we present an all-in-one and automatic approach, to be called SINATRA, that seeks to improve the usability of Tabular data through *Data annotation* (relying on an existing tool Mtab [12]) maps Tabular data elements to concepts in DBpedia KG to solve the issues of misspelling and missing or incomplete metadata. *Data repair* handles missing cell values in the Tabular data by fetching the corresponding concepts from DBpedia. *Data augmentation* allows the user to dynamically add the relevant columns and the corresponding cell values to the data. The evaluation results show that the SINATRA approach was able to annotate, repair, and augment the structured data.

In the near future, we plan to compare our proposal with other existing methods and tools, and extend it with additional features, such as (1) integrating additional knowledge graphs such as WikiData, LOV, Geonames and YAGO to improve the annotation, (2) evaluating the performance of our approach on other open datasets, (3) generating a RDF file of the annotated dataset to publish in Linked Open Data, and (4) providing a visualization graph to enhance the understanding on the relatedness between the concepts of the RDF file.

Acknowledgements. Rabeb Abida is funded by a CERUNA grant from the University of Namur, Belgium. Anthony Cleve is a professor in information system evolution at University of Namur, Belgium, where he heads the data-intensive system evolution lab. He is currently a visiting professor at Universitá della Svizzera italiana, Switzerland. Anthony is a member and former president of the PReCISE research center, and a member of the Namur Digital Institute (NADI). He co-edited the book "Evolving Software Systems", published by Springer in 2014.

References

1. Abdelmageed, N., Schindler, S.: JenTab meets SemTab 2021's new challenges. In: SemTab@ ISWC, pp. 42–53 (2021)
2. Abida, R., Belghith, E.H., Cleve, A.: An end-to-end framework for integrating and publishing linked open government data. In: 2020 IEEE 29th International Conference on Enabling Technologies: Infrastructure for Collaborative Enterprises (WETICE), pp. 257–262. IEEE (2020)
3. Auer, S., Bizer, C., Kobilarov, G., Lehmann, J., Cyganiak, R., Ives, Z.: DBpedia: a nucleus for a web of open data. In: Aberer, K., et al. (eds.) ASWC/ISWC -2007. LNCS, vol. 4825, pp. 722–735. Springer, Heidelberg (2007). https://doi.org/10.1007/978-3-540-76298-0_52

4. Azzi, R., et al.: AMALGAM: making tabular dataset explicit with knowledge graph. In: SemTab@ ISWC, pp. 9–16 (2020)
5. Benedetti, F., Bergamaschi, S., Po, L.: Online index extraction from linked open data sources. In: Second International Workshop on Linked Data for Information Extraction (LD4IE), vol. 1267, pp. 9–20. DEU (2014)
6. Chen, J., Jiménez-Ruiz, E., Horrocks, I., Sutton, C.: ColNet: embedding the semantics of web tables for column type prediction. In: Proceedings of the AAAI Conference on Artificial Intelligence, vol. 33, pp. 29–36 (2019)
7. Chen, J., Jiménez-Ruiz, E., Horrocks, I., Sutton, C.: Learning semantic annotations for tabular data. arXiv preprint arXiv:1906.00781 (2019)
8. Cremaschi, M., Avogadro, R., Chieregato, D.: MantisTable: an automatic approach for the semantic table interpretation. In: SemTab@ ISWC 2019, pp. 15–24 (2019)
9. Jiménez-Ruiz, E., Hassanzadeh, O., Efthymiou, V., Chen, J., Srinivas, K.: SemTab 2019: resources to benchmark tabular data to knowledge graph matching systems. In: Harth, A., et al. (eds.) ESWC 2020. LNCS, vol. 12123, pp. 514–530. Springer, Cham (2020). https://doi.org/10.1007/978-3-030-49461-2_30
10. Jiménez-Ruiz, E., Hassanzadeh, O., Efthymiou, V., Chen, J., Srinivas, K., Cutrona, V.: Results of SemTab 2020. In: CEUR Workshop Proceedings, vol. 2775, pp. 1–8 (2020)
11. Knap, T.: Towards odalic, a semantic table interpretation tool in the ADEQUATe project. In: LD4IE@ ISWC, pp. 26–37 (2017)
12. Nguyen, P., Kertkeidkachorn, N., Ichise, R., Takeda, H.: MTab: matching tabular data to knowledge graph using probability models. arXiv preprint arXiv:1910.00246 (2019)
13. Ongenae, F.: MAGIC: mining an augmented graph using INK, starting from a CSV (2021)
14. Roman, D., et al.: DataGraft: one-stop-shop for open data management. Semant. Web 9(4), 393–411 (2018)
15. Vrandečić, D., Krötzsch, M.: Wikidata: a free collaborative knowledgebase. Commun. ACM 57(10), 78–85 (2014)
16. Zhang, S., Balog, K.: Ad hoc table retrieval using semantic similarity. In: Proceedings of the 2018 World Wide Web Conference, pp. 1553–1562 (2018)

AI in Biological Applications and Medicine

Detecting Human Embryo Cleavage Stages Using YOLO V5 Object Detection Algorithm

Akriti Sharma[1](✉)(iD), Mette H. Stensen[5](iD), Erwan Delbarre[2](iD),
Momin Siddiqui[4](iD), Trine B. Haugen[2](iD), Michael A. Riegler[3](iD),
and Hugo L. Hammer[1,3](iD)

[1] Department of Computer Science, Faculty of Technology, Art and Design,
Oslo Metropolitan University, Oslo, Norway
akritish@oslomet.no
[2] Department of Life Sciences and Health, Faculty of Health Sciences,
Oslo Metropolitan University, Oslo, Norway
[3] Department of Holistic Systems, Simula Metropolitan Center for Digital
Engineering, Oslo, Norway
[4] Department of Computer Science, Jamia Millia Islamia, New Delhi, India
[5] Fertilitetssenteret, Embryology, Oslo, Norway

Abstract. Assisted reproductive technology (ART) refers to treatments of infertility which include the handling of eggs, sperm and embryos. The success of ART procedures depends on several factors, including the quality of the embryo transferred to the woman. The assessment of embryos is mostly based on the morphokinetic parameters of their development, which include the number of cells at a given time point indicating the cell stage and the duration of each cell stage. In many clinics, time-lapse imaging systems are used for continuous visual inspection of the embryo development. However, the analysis of time-lapse data still requires the evaluation, by embryologists, of the morphokinetic parameters and cleavage patterns, making the assessment subjective. Recently the application of object detection in the field of medical imaging enabled the accurate detection of lesion or object of interest. Motivated by this research direction, we proposed a methodology to detect and track cells present inside embryos in time-lapse image series. The methodology employed an object detection technique called YOLO v5 and annotated the start of observed cell stages based on the cell count. Our approach could identify cell division to detect cell cleavage or start of next cell stage accurately up to the 5-cell stage. The methodology also highlighted instances of embryos development with abnormal cell cleavage patterns. On an average the methodology used 8 s to annotate a video frame (20 frames per second), which will not pose any delay for the embryologists while assessing embryo quality. The results were validated by embryologists, and they considered the methodology as a useful tool for their clinical practice.

Keywords: Track cell division · Detect cell in human embryo · Detect cell cleavage stage · Object detection

© The Author(s) 2022
E. Zouganeli et al. (Eds.): NAIS 2022, CCIS 1650, pp. 81–93, 2022.
https://doi.org/10.1007/978-3-031-17030-0_7

1   Introduction

In Assisted Reproductive Technology (ART) procedures, eggs are fertilized out-
side the body. The fertilized eggs called embryos are cultivated in a controlled
environment before being transferred to the woman. The selection of an embryo
for transfer is based on the embryologist's evaluation of its quality. Embryos are
typically assessed using morphological features such as cell count being specific
to a cell stage or the size of the cells and the duration of the different cell stages
[5]. The morphokinetic parameters include the period of successive embryonic
cell divisions leading chronologically to the 2-cell stage (for two cells), 3-cell
stage (for three cells), 4-cell stage (for four cells), 5-cell stage, 6-cell stage, 7-cell
stage, 8-cell stage, 9+-cell stage and finally morula, which is a compacted structure made of small size cells in the range of 8—16 followed by blastocyst which
is made up of about hundred cells. The cell stages of embryo development are
shown in Fig. 1. The duration of different cell stages has proved to be significant
in evaluating the embryo quality [18]. A simple way for calculating the duration is by counting the number of cells and tracking cell division, which requires
the continuous monitoring of the developing embryo. The time-lapse technology
(TLT) systems now used in many clinics are capable of providing digital images
of embryos at frequent time intervals [14]. In a vast majority of cases, the output from TLT systems is still analysed by embryologists who manually annotate
morphological features, abnormal cleavage pattern that are correlated to embryo
quality [6] and duration of cell stages, thus introducing intra- and interobserver
variability [17]. Some TLT systems though, allow computer-assisted annotation
which might reduce the intra- and interobserver variability among embryologists
[9], but the usage of the feature can incur additional costs. Recently, the application of object detection algorithms in the field of medical imaging has proven
to provide fast and accurate results [10, 12].

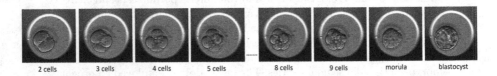

2 cells   3 cells   4 cells   5 cells   8 cells   9 cells   morula   blastocyst

Fig. 1. Cell stages of human embryo development.

In this study, we have developed an approach to locate cells in the images
depicting embryonic development. The approach was developed and evaluated
based on TLT images. The images were the frames of TLT videos. The suggested
approach was able to count the number of cells in each TLT frame, track the
detected cells and cell divisions in consecutive frames. Our approach also identified different cell stages. The suggested approach employed YOLO v5 to detect
cells present in the frames. The approach further tracked each individual cell
across different cell stages by marking each cell boundary with distinct colored

circular overlays. The distinct color scheme helped the embryologists in tracking individual cells, their cell divisions and identifying cell cleavages over the course of the TLT video. The average processing time taken by our approach was 8 s for a TLT video. The methodology could also detect abnormal cleavage pattern such as direct cleavage [16] and reverse cleavage [11].

We used six performance metric to evaluate the software's performance in detecting cell stages and the software performed best for 2-cell stage detection and the performance was reducing with increase in the number of cells inside the embryo. The performance of our method was validated by embryologists and they considered tracking of cells with colored overlays as useful. The main contributions of this study were: (i) Using our method, the embryologists could accurately detect cells, track cell divisions and determine cell cleavage stages up to 5 cells; (ii) our approach has the potential for detecting abnormal cleavage patterns in human embryo development; and (iii) this approach could generate accurate annotations for the morphokinetics related to cell cleavages and cell-stages in 8 s for TLT videos with the frame rate of 20 on an average.

2   Methods and Materials

2.1   Data

The dataset was collected retrospectively at Fertilitetssenteret, a fertility clinic in Oslo, Norway, and consisted of TLT videos of human embryo development. The embryos were cultured inside a time-lapse system called Embryoscope^{TM} (Vitrolife, Denmark).

Time-Lapse Imaging. The introduction of TLT in ART practices enables continuous monitoring of embryos throughout their whole culture period. Embryoscope^{TM} is an incubator equipped with an inbuilt microscope and a camera. For each embryo placed inside the incubator, the system took 8-bit images at several focal planes (number varying between 3 or 5) between every 10–15 min. Each 8-bit image has a resolution of 500×500 pixels. By using time-lapse imaging (TLI) images, embryologists gets insights into the morphokinetics associated with the embryo cell development without removing embryos from the incubators [7]. Later for every TLT video the embryologists analyzed each video's frame (8-bit image) and manually annotated starting of an observed cell-stage. The observed cell stages were as: 2-cell, 3-cell, 4-cell, 5-cell, 8-cell, 9^{+}-cell, morula and blastocyst. In this study, we used 890 TLT videos from which we extracted the frames corresponding to the annotated start of a cell cleavage stages. It resulted in total of 2785 images and each cell stage had 350 images except for Blastocyst with 335 images. We denoted this as Dataset I and used it to train the object detection algorithm. A second dataset, Dataset II, was also created comprising of 11 other TLT videos. We annotated this dataset for the start of observed cell-stages using our methodology. Dataset II was used as an independent dataset.

Abnormal Cleavage Patterns. A successful fertilization between sperm and egg results in a fertilized egg which over next few days undergoes a series of cell division progressing through the cell stages. The embryo should cleaves every 12 or 24 h. Thus, by the time an embryo has reached Day 3 of development, it should be between four and eight cells. [1]. The continuous monitoring of embryo morphology using TLT revealed certain abnormal cell cleavage pattern [4]. One such pattern is reverse cleavage which is defined as a decrease in the number of cell during cell division. This means that cells in a cell stage fused together to form a cell (reducing cell count) and they cleaved again after that [11]. Another abnormal cleavage pattern is direct cleavage which occurs when a cell divides directly into three more daughter cells [16]. Such abnormal cleavages correlate with impaired embryo development and implantation potential [13,19] and should be detected.

Ethical Consideration. A fully anonymized data was collected after the approval by Regional Committee for Medical and Health Research Ethics - South East Norway (REC). All experiments were performed in accordance with the guidelines and regulations of REC, and the General Data Protection Regulations.

2.2   Object Detection

Object detection is fundamental task in image processing. It is a form of image classification where method predict objects in an image using bounding boxes around the objects. It is referred as the detection and localization of objects in an image, where the objects belong to predefined classes [2]. In recent years, due to contribution of deep learning (DL), and especially convolutional neural network (CNN), object detection models outperforms specifically in field of medical imaging [12]. The convolutional kernels in the models extract features, layer by layer and obtain the probabilities of candidate bounding boxes belonging to different classes. The object detection models can be categorised as: one stage network such as You Only Look Once (YOLO) [15] and two stage network such as Fast R-CNN [8]. A two stage object detection model breaks down object detection into two task, first detects possible object region and then classify the image in those regions into predefined classes [2]. Whereas, YOLO as a one stage network, proposes the use of an end-to-end neural network that processes the whole picture by dividing it into N grids with equal dimensional region. Each of these grids predicts the probability of object classes being present in the grid along with object label and bounding box coordinates relative to grid's cell coordinates. The bounding boxes are weighted by the expected probability of each object. Then, YOLO using non maximal suppression technique to suppress all bounding boxes with lower probability scores. YOLO uses the metric mean Average Precision (mAP) for measuring the decision performance while predicting bounding boxes for object classes. mAP is the mean of the Average Precision (AP) for all object classes. AP is the summary of the precision-sensitivity curve for YOLO v5 predicting bounding box per object class into a single value that provides average of all precision values [2]. If we want to apply object detection in real time videos at fertility clinic, algorithm speed should be fast. YOLO is a much faster algorithm than its counterparts [2]. Thus, in this study, we used YOLO v5 to detect object classes: cell, morula and blastocyst in the frames of TLI videos. The annotated location of the object classes in the training images (Dataset I) and YOLO v5 predictions on Dataset I were reviewed by embryologists. The mAP for object cell was 0.65, morula 0.78 and for blastocyst was 0.80.

2.3 Colored Circular Overlay Algorithm

In this section we explained the suggested algorithm to add colored circular overlay to embryo cells. Our approach first used YOLO v5 to detect cells present in frames of TLI videos. Once we got bounding boxes or coordinates for the detected cells, then we used OpenCV library to mark each cell boundary with different colored circular overlay. After detecting cells with distinct colored overlay, the methodology computed the cell count and recorded coordinates for each cell. The assigned color to a cell was maintained until the cell divided into daughter cells. Later, each daughter cell got a distinct coloured overlay for itself. The methodology recognized the daughter cells as unique individual cells and kept track of them in the succeeding frames using the color of the overlay. After processing the whole TLI videos, the methodology provided a new version of the input TLI video, where the frames had colored overlays on detected cell boundaries in each video frames.

If cell count remained same between consecutive frames, for the current frame, our methodology calculated proximity between each cell in the current frame to the cells detected in the preceding frame. The proximity was calculated using the difference between the coordinates of two cells, the first cell from the current frame and the second cell from preceding frame. If the calculated proximity lay within a specific threshold, the methodology copied color scheme of the cells from preceding frame to the cells in current frame. This way cell tracking using colored overlays was performed. The proximity threshold used in our algorithm was 0.10 for cell count less than 4, 0.05 for count greater than 4.

If cell count differed between consecutive frames, our methodology checked whether the current frame has higher cell count than the preceding frame. If true, then there was a possibility that one of the cell might have cleaved into daughter cells. The methodology detected the parent cell from preceding frame using same concept of proximity and assigned color of parent to daughter cells recognizing the frame with cell division. The methodology, then, annotated the current frame as the start of cleavage of a cell-stage. The cell-stage was corresponding to the number of detected cells. If false, or the cell count for the current frame being lower than the cell count of preceding frame, the methodology still calculated proximity between cells and copied the matching color scheme. The lower count the for current frame could be case of abnormal cleavage or few cells not being detected by YOLO v5.

3   Results

To test our methodology we used Dataset II for cell tracking and detecting cell cleavage stages. The methodology processed each video in the dataset and generated a corresponding video with colored circular overlays on detected cells in every video frame. The embryologists could track a cell using the color of overlay for that cell. Starting from the first frame, our methodology assigned distinct color to each cell and that color was maintained up until the cell divided. Then the daughter cells were also assigned different color overlays from the next frame. In Fig. 2, we present few frames extracted from a video generated by our methodology present in the bottom row. The top row shows actual video frames. The frames in the bottom row, have colored circular overlay marking the boundary of detected cell and same color scheme is maintained until cell division. The cell division can be seen in frame 5 and 7 of Fig. 2 and distinct colored overlay for each cell in the succeeding frames 6 and 8 of Fig. 2.

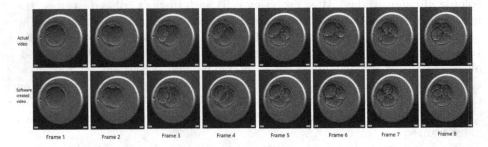

Fig. 2. Extracted frames from TLI video of embryo development til 4-cell stage. The top row shows actual video frames and the bottom row shows our method's output with colored overlay on each cell. In frame 1, single cell divided into 2 cell as shown in frame 3 and 4. The yellow colored cell divided in frame 5. From frame 6, our method annotated 3-cell stage, each cell with distinct color. The blue colored cell starts to divide in frame 7 and 4-cell stage was annotated from frame 8. (Color figure online)

3.1   Comparison with Embryologists

Two embryologists independently validated the performance of our methodology. To this end, they verified the number of detected cells, in each frame of the generated videos. They also verified that the starting of cell stage, as annotated by the methodology, was either exact match to their annotation or varied by only a few frames on average. It was observed that our methodology detected cells, tracked cell division and precisely annotated the start of each cell stage up up to 5-cell one. For stages with cell count above five, the annotated start of cleavage was later than actual by 9 to 10 frames on an average. In Fig. 3 we present some frames extracted from a video with embryo development til 9-cell stage. Our methodology could detect cells and tracked cell divisions accurately up up to 5 cell-stage, as seen from frames 1 to 8 of Fig. 3. When cell count exceeded five the methodology confused between overlapping cell boundaries and either missed detecting a cell (frame 12 of Fig. 3) or detected incorrect location for cell (yellow circle in frame 9 of Fig. 3).

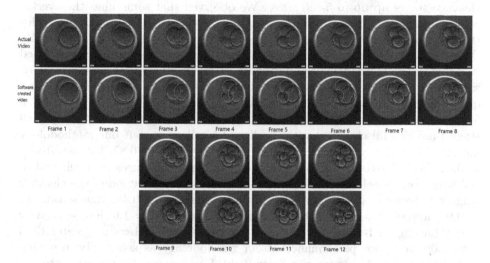

Fig. 3. Extracted frames from TLI video of embryo development til 9-cell stage. The top row shows actual video frames and the bottom row shows our method's output with colored overlay on each cell. The green colored cell divided in frame 4. From frame 5, our method annotated it as 3-cell stage and tracked the cell division from frame 6: blue colored overlay. The 4-cell stage was annotated in frame 7. In frame 9, incorrect cell location was detected: yellow overlay but correct cell count was detected in frame 10 and 11. Again, a cell was missed in frame 12. (Color figure online)

3.2 Cell Counting Performance

Next, we evaluated the performance of our methodology using the following six performance metrics: sensitivity (SENS), precision (PREC), specificity (SPEC), accuracy (ACC), F1-score (F1), and the Matthews correlation coefficient (MCC). Using multiple metrics provides a more reliable and robust insight into the real capabilities of our approach. We measured the efficiency of the methodology in reporting the correct cell count in a frame, tracking of cell division and annotating the start of a cell cleavage stage. The results were validated by the embryologists using the criteria based on cell count, detected cell boundary, for cell division picking correct parent for the daughter cells and matching our methodology's annotation with their annotation for the start of a cell-stage. The metric MCC is a reliable statistical rate giving high scores only if the prediction (frame belonging to a cell stage) obtained good results in all of the four confusion matrix categories [3]. MCC measures the difference between actual label (frame annotated by embryologist for belonging to a cell stage) and predicted label (frame annotated by our methodology for belonging to a cell stage). A

MCC value lies between -1 to 1. A negative MCC value indicates that there is no agreement between actual and predicted label. While MCC value around zero indicates model decides randomly and a value above zero indicates correct prediction. Our methodology obtained an MCC of 0.77 for predicting start of cleavage stages up up to 5-cell stage. We observed that sometimes the overlay color changes for cells abruptly between frames or wrong parent was chosen for the daughter cells. We labelled these predictions as incorrect. Next, to quantify the performance of our methodology we used the performance metrics as listed in Table 1. The methodology performed best for 2-cell stage (precision = 0.91, sensitivity = 0.98, highest F1-score = 0.95). The detectiom of 1-cell stage was quite accurate (precision = 0.99, sensitivity = 0.86, high F1-score = 0.91) but, a few instances of 1-cell stage were misclassified as morula. A few instances of 4-cell stage were also misclassified with 3-cell and 5-cell stage, but our methodology mostly detected 4-cell stage accurately (high precision = 0.87, low sensitivity = 0.62, high F1-score = 0.73). A higher number of instances of 3-cell and 5-cell stage were misclassified with other stages, still the detection of the cleavage stage was better than random: 3-cell (average precision = 0.46, high sensitivity = 0.93, average F1-score = 0.61), 5-cell (high precision = 1.0, low sensitivity = 0.31, average F1-score = 0.47). For cell stages with cell count greater than 5 we observed poor performance of our methodology as sensitivity, precision and F1-score for the stages was below 0.40. Further, we did not evaluate our methodology for these cell stages.

Table 1. Evaluation results of the performance metrics on Dataset II for detecting embryo cell cleavage stages using our methodology

Cell stage	Recall	Precision	Specificity	Accuracy	F1-score
1-cell stage	0.86	0.99	0.99	0.93	0.91
2-cell stage	0.98	0.94	0.98	0.98	0.96
3-cell stage	0.93	0.46	0.92	0.92	0.61
4-cell stage	0.62	0.87	0.62	0.91	0.73
5-cell stage	0.31	1.0	0.31	0.98	0.47
6-cell stage	0.38	0.14	0.84	0.93	0.20
7-cell stage	0.27	0.16	0.83	0.90	0.19
8-cell stage	0.38	0.36	0.89	0.81	0.37
9-cell stage	0.20	0.41	0.89	0.81	0.35

We observed the similar pattern in the receiver operating characteristic (ROC) curve for cell stages up upto 5-cell stages. As shown in Fig. 4 the area under the curve (AUC) is maximum for 2-cell stage and minimum for 5-cell stage. Thus, our methodology performed best in detecting and tracking cell division for 2-cell stage and is worst for 5-cell stage.

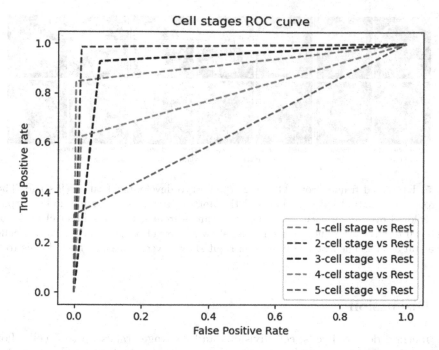

Fig. 4. ROC curve for the software detecting embryo cell cleavage stages on Dataset II.

3.3 Computational Efficiency

We also calculated the processing time taken by our methodology. The processing time included the duration for video processing and generating its corresponding video with colored overlays on Dataset II. On an average 8 s were required. If we divide Dataset II into two groups: (i) A: videos upto 5-cell stage. (ii) B: videos having cell stage with cell count greater than five. Our methodology, for A reported 4 s and for B reported 19 s as an average processing time. The average number of processed frames per second (fps) for videos in Dataset II was 20, 8 fps for A and 33 fps for B. This is far quicker than the real-time progression of embryos, and the processing time do not pose any practical delay for the embryologists using the method for embryo assessment.

3.4 Anomaly Detection

We further evaluated whether our method could detect anomalies in the embryo development. In Dataset II, there were two TLI videos with instances of direct cleavage and reverse cleavage. Figure 5 shows frames from one of these video where our method detected anomalies. For direct cleavage the single cell divided into 3 cells. Reverse cleavage was observed on 3-cell stage (2 cells fused into one and later divided again into 2 cells) and 4-cell stage (2 cells fused into one cell). The abnormal cleavage pattern detected by our methodology was validated by the embryologists as correct detection.

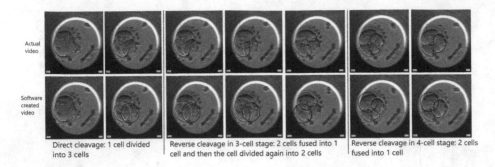

Direct cleavage: 1 cell divided into 3 cells

Reverse cleavage in 3-cell stage: 2 cells fused into 1 cell and then the cell divided again into 2 cells

Reverse cleavage in 4-cell stage: 2 cells fused into 1 cell

Fig. 5. Extracted frames from TLI video of embryo development til 4-cell stage. The top row shows actual video frames and the bottom row shows our method's output with colored overlay on each cell. First two frames from left shows direct cleavage of single cell to 3 cells. The next three frames show reverse cleavage from 3 cells to 2 cells and again 3 cells. The last two frames on right show reverse cleavage from 4 cells to 3 cells.

4   Discussion

Our method detected cells, cell divisions and cleavage stages up to 5 cells. For single cell or 1-cell stage detection, it performed with high precision, but also misclassification with the stage morula was observed. This could be attributed to the compacted structure of morula that has high resemblance to 1-cell stage. Our approach performed best in the detection of 2-cell stage, and the performance reduced on much higher scale while detecting cells or reporting cell stages having cell count greater than five. The methodology detected those cell stages later than their actual cleavage and it was because of increased overlapping between neighbouring cell boundaries. With the higher cell count, the structure of a cell-stage gets more complex and cells tend to lie on top of each other, making cell counting more difficult. The methodology considered two cells as one because YOLO v5 is trained to analyse a 2-D image and the depth information (3-D view) directing towards potential overlap is missing. We observed that for cell stages three and five, there were high fluctuation in reported values for the performance indicators such as sensitivity and precision. 3-cell stage had lower precision and higher sensitivity while the 5-cell stage had lower sensitivity and higher precision. For these stages, the imbalance in the performance of our approach was because the overlay's color changed for cells abruptly between the frames.

Once a cell stage was detected using our approach, in the consecutive frames less number of cells were detected by YOLO v5, and then again the correct count was reported. Thus, the training dataset for object detection need to be more comprehensive. If there is some noise in the images or some situations that are not covered by the training data, the robustness of the object detection model will be reduced [12]. Our methodology was time efficient and could generate videos with colored overlays with annotated cell stages in 8 s on average for Dataset II videos with 20 fps on average. In comparison, the camera in time-lapse incubator captures images of an embryo after 10–15 min. This shows that the inclusion of our methodology to process TLT videos will not bear any additional time delay and will support embryologist in decision making. Thus, our approach can be included in real time.

The methodology can help in reducing the subjectivity associated with the assessment of an embryo's quality. The methodology also proved potential for detecting abnormal cleavage pattern which can be useful for embryologist while assessing embryo's quality and viability to be transferred to female body.

5 Conclusion

Object detection proved to be pragmatic for ART. Overall, our approach successfully detected cells, effectively tracked cell divisions and accurately determined cleavage stages up up to 5 cell-stage. Our approach was time efficient and can be used in the real time processing of TLI videos without introducing an additional time delay. Tracking cell division using our methodology seems to have potential for detecting abrupt cleavage patterns such as direct or reverse cleavage. Qualitative evaluation by embryologists resulted in the overall verdict that the methodology is useful and seems promising for clinical practice. We also hypothesise that using a larger dataset for training and including images from other focal planes, to provide depth information, will enable our methodology to detect overlapping cells and cell cleavage stages with cell count greater than five.

References

1. Angeles, P.F.C.L.: Day 3 vs. day 5 embryo transfers (2019). https://www.pfcla.com/blog/day-3-vs-day-5-embryo-transfer
2. Bandyopadhyay, H.: Yolo: Real-time object detection explained (2022). https://www.v7labs.com/blog/yolo-object-detection
3. Chicco, D., Jurman, G.: The advantages of the Matthews correlation coefficient (MCC) over f1 score and accuracy in binary classification evaluation. BMC Genomics **21**, 6 (2020). https://doi.org/10.1186/s12864-019-6413-7
4. Cimadomo, D., et al.: P-210 abnormal cleavage patterns during embryo preimplantation development and their effect on blastulation: an overview from IVF patients with multiple IVF cycles in a time-lapse incubator. Human Reprod. **36**(Supplement_1), 230–231 (2021). https://doi.org/10.1093/humrep/deab130.209
5. Cummins, J.M., Breen, T.M., Harrison, K.L., Shaw, J.M., Wilson, L.M., Hennessey, J.F.: A formula for scoring human embryo growth rates in in vitro fertilization: its value in predicting pregnancy and in comparison with visual estimates of embryo quality. J. In Vitro Fert Embryo Transf. **3**(5), 284–295 (1986). https://doi.org/10.1186/s12938-019-0738-y
6. Desai, N., Goldberg, J.M., Austin, C., Falcone, T.: Are cleavage anomalies, multinucleation, or specific cell cycle kinetics observed with time-lapse imaging predictive of embryo developmental capacity or ploidy? Fertility Sterility **109**(4), 665–674 (2018). https://doi.org/10.1016/j.fertnstert.2017.12.025, https://www.sciencedirect.com/science/article/pii/S0015028217321726

7. Gallego, R.D., Remohí, J., Meseguer, M.: Time-lapse imaging: the state of the art[†]. Biol. Reprod. **101**(6), 1146–1154 (2019). https://doi.org/10.1093/biolre/ioz035
8. Girshick, R.: Fast R-CNN. In: 2015 IEEE International Conference on Computer Vision (ICCV), pp. 1440–1448 (2015). https://doi.org/10.1109/ICCV.2015.169
9. Kaser, D.J., Racowsky, C.: Clinical outcomes following selection of human preimplantation embryos with time-lapse monitoring: a systematic review. Human Reprod. Update **20**(5), 617–631 (2014). https://doi.org/10.1093/humupd/dmu023
10. Kaur, A., Singh, Y., Neeru, N., Kaur, L., Singh, A.: A survey on deep learning approaches to medical images and a systematic look up into real-time object detection. Arch. Comput. Methods Eng. **29**, 2071–2111 (2021). https://doi.org/10.1007/s11831-021-09649-9
11. Li, F., Abozaid, T., et al.: Multinucleation on 2-cell stage and reverse cleavage may not impact implantation outcomes: a time-lapse study. Fertility Sterility **102**, E135 (2014). https://doi.org/10.1016/j.fertnstert.2014.07.461
12. Li, Z., Dong, M., Wen, S., Hu, X., Zhou, P., Zeng, Z.: CLU-CNNs: object detection for medical images. Neurocomputing **350**, 53–59 (2019). https://doi.org/10.1016/j.neucom.2019.04.028
13. Liu, Y., Chapple, V., Roberts, P., Matson, P.: Prevalence, consequence, and significance of reverse cleavage by human embryos viewed with the use of the embryoscope time-lapse video system. Fertility Sterility **102**, 1295–1300 (2014). https://doi.org/10.1016/j.fertnstert.2014.07.1235
14. Paulson, R.J.: Time-lapse imaging. Fertility Sterility **109**(4), 583 (2018). https://doi.org/10.1016/j.fertnstert.2018.02.013, https://www.sciencedirect.com/science/article/pii/S001502821830089X
15. Redmon, J., Divvala, S., Girshick, R., Farhadi, A.: You only look once: unified, real-time object detection. In: 2016 IEEE Conference on Computer Vision and Pattern Recognition (CVPR), pp. 779–788 (2016). https://doi.org/10.1109/CVPR.2016.91
16. Rubio, I., et al.: Limited implantation success of direct-cleaved human zygotes: a time-lapse study. Fertility Sterility **98**, 1458–1463 (2012). https://doi.org/10.1016/j.fertnstert.2012.07.1135
17. Storr, A., Venetis, C.A., Cooke, S., Kilani, S., Ledger, W.: Inter-observer and intra-observer agreement between embryologists during selection of a single Day 5 embryo for transfer: a multicenter study. Human Reprod. **32**(2), 307–314 (2017). https://doi.org/10.1093/humrep/dew330
18. Wong, C., et al.: Non-invasive imaging of human embryos before embryonic genome activation predicts development to the blastocyst stage. Nat. Biotechnol. **28**, 1115–1121 (2010). https://doi.org/10.1038/nbt.1686
19. Zaninovic, N., Ye, Z., Zhan, Q., Clarke, R., Rosenwaks, Z.: Cell stage onsets, embryo developmental potential and chromosomal abnormalities in embryos exhibiting direct unequal cleavages (DUCs). Fertility Sterility **100**, S242 (2013). https://doi.org/10.1016/j.fertnstert.2013.07.1223

Phenotyping of Cervical Cancer Risk Groups via Generalized Low-Rank Models Using Medical Questionnaires

Florian Becker[1,2(✉)], Mari Nygård[3], Jan Nygård[3], Age Smilde[1,4], and Evrim Acar[1]

[1] Simula Metropolitan Center for Digital Engineering, Oslo, Norway
florian@simula.no
[2] Oslo Metropolitan University, Oslo, Norway
[3] Cancer Registry of Norway, Oslo, Norway
[4] Swammerdam Institute for Life Sciences, University of Amsterdam, Amsterdam, Netherlands

Abstract. The purpose of this study is to uncover cervical cancer (CC) risk phenotypes from self-reported lifestyle questionnaires and screening data. In general, computational phenotype discovery aims to find subgroups among individuals that share distinctive characteristics by analyzing electronic health records (EHR). This can benefit the understanding of a disease as well as uncover risk factors and provide possibilities for preventive action. The features in the *women* ($n = 6359$) by *questionnaire features* ($p = 29$) matrix with missing data are of different statistical data types (e.g., binary or ordinal data). We use so-called *generalized low-rank models* (GLRM) that can address this challenge via different statistical-data-type-dependent loss functions. We show that these models can uncover phenotypes related to cervical cancer risk factors from large-scale questionnaire data.

Keywords: Computational phenotyping · Unsupervised learning · Low-rank approximations · Electronic health records · Cervical cancer

1 Introduction

The collection and processing of electronic health records (EHR) has the potential to increase the quality of care and diagnostic value [1,2]. EHR may include, for instance, the medical history, medication, demographics, or other personal or lifestyle meta information. Questionnaires or surveys are one way to gather information about lifestyle choices that might serve as complementary information to other EHR data. Anticipating the adoption of EHR, suitable data mining methods are needed to analyze EHR data and uncover different patient subgroups or *phenotypes* [3]. By design, questionnaires typically include aspects that are assumed or known to be risk factors. The incidence of a disease can be compared by conducting hypothesis tests between different predefined groups, for

E. Zouganeli et al. (Eds.): NAIS 2022, CCIS 1650, pp. 94–110, 2022.
https://doi.org/10.1007/978-3-031-17030-0_8

instance, between smokers and non-smokers. However, in order to uncover previously unknown phenotypes of patients, unsupervised multivariate approaches are needed. Low-rank matrix factorizations, such as principal component analysis (PCA) [4,5] or nonnegative matrix factorization (NMF) [6], are promising tools to analyze multivariate data and reveal underlying patterns in an unsupervised way. These approaches have the advantage of not presuming any kind of groups. Thus, they may allow to discover patient phenotypes and co-factors, i.e., features that co-occur.

However, missing data and different statistical data types of feature columns are challenging problems when analyzing heterogeneous (questionnaire) data. Generalized low-rank models (GLRM) provide a promising framework that was developed recently to address these challenges [7,8]. In this context, generalization stands for the extension of losses beyond the standard quadratic loss. GLRM approximates a heterogeneous data matrix using low-rank score and loading matrices by taking into account the statistical data type of each column. We investigate this idea, and explore whether there is a benefit for computational phenotyping compared to an NMF-based model *agnostic* to data types.

1.1   Cervical Cancer Screening Programme

Since establishing a coordinated nationwide cervical cancer screening programme in Norway in 1995 the incidence of the disease was substantially reduced [9]. In addition to collecting the screening results, the Cancer Registry Norway sent out a questionnaire to roughly 30,000 women in 2004–2005 and 2011–2012 [10,11]. It comprises questions about lifestyle choices such as drinking and smoking habits as well as questions about contraception usage, sexual activity (e.g., number of sexual partners) and previous history of sexually transmitted diseases (STDs), among others. Together with the screening results from a cytology examination, this data set can provide researchers as well as medical practitioners with valuable insights about demographics, disease progression and patient phenotypes. The complete screening history of a woman f can be denoted by $\{(s_i, d_i)\}_{i=1}^{n_f}$, where s_i is the age at the i-th screening, d_i is the associated examination result, encoded by diagnosis codes (see Table 1, Appendix) and n_f is the total number of screenings for f. The (cytological or histological) examination results range from no atypical cells to different categorizations of pre-cancers and cancers. While the screening data is a population-level data set, the questionnaire data covers only a sub-population.

1.2   Uncovering Phenotypes and Co-Factors is Ongoing Research

While it is known that the human papillomavirus (HPV) causes nearly all cervical cancer cases, different risk factors for such an infection and their interaction among each other are still a relevant topic. Previous studies and reviews have identified various factors that increase the risk of cervical cancer, e.g., the duration of hormonal contraception [12] or the marital status [13]. Early age at first intercourse as well as early pregnancies have been determined to be risk factors in developing countries [14]. A further study has proposed a model according to which the incidence rate of cervical cancer is proportional to the square of time since first intercourse [15]. Some factors, such as smoking, have been identified as *co-factors*, meaning that it increases the cervical cancer risk among HPV positive women [16]. In order to reveal these statistical associations, studies typically use uni- or bivariate tests [17]. However, to uncover more complex phenotypes, multivariate approaches are needed.

In this study, we use GLRMs to analyze a large-scale medical questionnaire data set linked with screening data, and show that GLRMs are a viable method for phenotype discovery in the context of cervical cancer risk groups. We demonstrate that when GLRMs are used to analyze questionnaire data in the form of a *female participants* by *features* matrix, meaningful phenotypes showing statistically significant differences between risk-level subgroups are revealed. One phenotype, for instance, is characterized by the number of sexual partners as well as hormonal contraception usage. Some extracted phenotypes are consistent across models using different number of components. Grouping women based on a phenotype description can potentially be used in the future to personalize cervical cancer screening programs. The ultimate goal is to avoid both too infrequent screening and over-screening. While low-rank models have been used previously for phenotyping EHR data [1,2,18,19] primarily focusing on the analysis of medication, procedure and diagnosis data, the multivariate analysis of self-reported medical questionnaires to reveal phenotypes remains an under-researched and challenging problem.

This study, to the best of our knowledge, presents the first attempt to discover phenotypes from survey data that was collected within a cervical cancer screening programme, using NMF as well as a low-rank model with data-type-specific loss functions.

2   Materials and Methods

2.1   Questionnaire Description and Preprocessing

The aspects that are covered in the questionnaire can be roughly grouped into nine categories: contraception, awareness of HPV, smoking, drinking habits, sexual activity, pregnancies, previous STDs and other personal information like marital status and education. The answers to these questions have different *statistical data types*. A question of Boolean type, for example, asks for whether a person smokes, while a further question asks for the age when the person started (or stopped) smoking. In addition to this categorization of feature columns according to their statistical data type, the features can also be categorized according to their *static* or *dynamic* nature. Static features, once reported, do not change over time (e.g., if hormonal contraception was ever used before), while dynamic features (e.g., the number of years of smoking) are time-dependent. To a certain extent, the design of the questionnaire allows to associate the questionnaire features with screening results.

By recording the starting age of a certain habit or the onset of a certain kind of contraception use, the time since the starting age can be computed at a certain later screening time point s_i.

For each screening s_i, a subset of the questionnaire features are transformed such that they denote durations or "time since onset". These features are also called *delta-time* features, and the prefix dt_ is used to denote them. Delta features allow examination results $d_1, \ldots, d_{n_f}$ to be associated with questionnaire feature vectors.

Transformed features can only be computed if the starting point for a certain habit lies in the past, given a certain screening time point s_i. Questionnaire feature rows that do not fulfill this condition are discarded.

To arrive at the final questionnaire data, the feature vector corresponding to the *worst* screening result (diagnosis codes in ascending order, cf. Table 1 in the Appendix) for each female participant is extracted. Rows and feature columns in the data set that contained more than 50% missing values were discarded. For example, questions about different STDs (e.g., chlamydia, gonorrhea) were only answered by relatively few women. The final features that were included in the analysis are shown in Table 3, Appendix. Screening results are heavily skewed towards normals. In order to prevent any low-rank model to primarily model the normal group, only a randomly sampled subset of normals is used. The distribution of risk-level categories in the final matrix in the form of a *women* ($n = 6359$) by *questionnaire items/features* ($p = 29$) matrix is shown in Table 1, Appendix.

2.2   Generalized Low-Rank Models

Notation: Scalars are denoted as lowercase letters, vectors as boldface lowercase letters, and matrices as boldface uppercase letters. By x_{ij} we denote the (i, j) entry of a matrix $\mathbf{X}$. We use $\mathbf{x}_{i:}$ to denote the ith row and $\mathbf{x}_{:j}$ to denote jth column of an $n \times p$ matrix $\mathbf{X}$. We treat both $\mathbf{x}_{i:}$ and $\mathbf{x}_{:j}$ as column vectors.

We use generalized low-rank models to approximate the heterogeneous survey data matrix $\mathbf{Q} \in \mathbb{R}^{n \times p}$ using low-rank female-mode matrix $\mathbf{X} \in \mathbb{R}^{n \times k}$ and a phenotype matrix $\mathbf{Y} \in \mathbb{R}^{k \times p}$ with k factors, where k is often much smaller than $\min(n, p)$. In contrast to data matrix $\mathbf{Q}$, factor matrices $\mathbf{X}$ and $\mathbf{Y}$ are real-valued. The factor matrices are computed by solving the following optimization problem:

$$\min_{\mathbf{X}, \mathbf{Y}} \quad \sum_{(i,j) \in \Omega} \mathcal{L}_j(q_{ij}, \mathbf{x}_{i:}^\top \mathbf{y}_{:j}) / \sigma_j^2 + \lambda_r \mathcal{R}_r(\mathbf{X}) + \lambda_c \mathcal{R}_c(\mathbf{Y}) \tag{1}$$

$$\text{s.t.} \qquad\qquad\qquad\qquad \mathbf{X} \geq 0, \mathbf{Y} \geq 0,$$

where Ω is the set of observed entries, $\mathcal{L}_j : (\mathbb{R} \times \mathbb{R}) \rightarrow \mathbb{R}$ denotes the entry-wise loss function that is dependent on statistical data type of the respective column in $\mathbf{Q}$, and $\mathbf{X} \geq 0$ indicates that all matrix entries are nonnegative. To balance the unequal scaling across different columns, $\sigma_j^2 = \frac{1}{n_j - 1} \sum_{i:(i,j) \in \Omega} \mathcal{L}_j(\mu_j, q_{ij})$ is introduced, where $\mu_j = \text{argmin}_\mu \sum_{i:(i,j) \in \Omega} \mathcal{L}_j(\mu, q_{ij})$ which is a generalization of the variance that is dependent on the loss function, where n_j denotes the number of non-missing entries in column j. This means that scaling is not a preprocessing step, instead in order to scale the columns, a small optimization problem needs to be solved to get the $\{\mu_j\}_{j=1}^p$, which are then used to compute $\{\sigma_j^2\}_{j=1}^p$. The $\{\mu_j\}_{j=1}^p$ itself are not used in the optimization problem (1), i.e., the columns are only scaled, but not centered. $\mathcal{R}_r(\mathbf{X}) = \sum_{i=1}^n r_i(\mathbf{x}_{i:})$ and $\mathcal{R}_c(\mathbf{X}) = \sum_{j=1}^p r_j(\mathbf{y}_{:j})$ denote regularization terms across rows and columns, denoted by the subscripts r and c, respectively. We use the ℓ_1-norm, i.e., $r_i(\mathbf{x}_{i:}) = \|\mathbf{x}_{i:}\|_1 = \sum_{j=1}^k |x_{ij}|$ to enforce sparsity across the rows of $\mathbf{X}$ and columns of $\mathbf{Y}$. The reasons for using sparsity are two-fold: Sparsity enforces clustering [20, 21] and (together with non-negativity) a less-arbitrary, more well-posed solution of the optimization problem above. In general, low-rank models are non-convex. Missing data exacerbate the problem of non-convexity and lead to more local minima [22]. Note that the formulation above does not incorporate a weight matrix. Instead, the set Ω contains indices of all available data in $\mathbf{Q}$. An equivalent formulation is to use a binary weight matrix that encodes missing and non-missing data.

Low-rank approximations have been extended beyond the minimization of the quadratic loss in the past, e.g., to model Poisson or Bernoulli-distributed data [23]. The framework used in this study, however, facilitates the use of different loss functions as well as imposing constraints on the factors through regularization. Constraints play a crucial role in matrix factorizations since additional constraints are often needed to reveal unique patterns (that can be further interpreted as, e.g., phenotypes, biomarkers). The framework has been used before to investigate autism spectrum disorder phenotypes using hospitalization records [7].

3   Experiments

We assess the performance of a GLRM-based model in terms of revealing phenotypes from the questionnaire data matrix $\mathbf{Q}$. Our results demonstrate that GLRM can reveal phenotypes showing statistically significant differences between cervical cancer risk groups. We also show that both GLRM and an NMF-based model find similar *general risk factors* using a 4-component model. However, when high number of components is used to reveal more phenotypes, GLRM uncovers more phenotypes that are both statistically significant and consistent.

3.1   Implementation Details and Experimental Set-Up

In order to solve the optimization problem given in (1), we use the Julia package LowRankModels.jl that fits low-rank models using an alternating proximal gradient method [8]. We extended this framework to fit our needs. For instance, we implemented a Kullback-Leibler divergence loss function $\mathcal{L}_{\mathrm{KL}}$ for count data (cf. Table 2 in the Appendix). To avoid local minima, we use 50 random initializations and the one returning the minimum loss is used. We also validate the uniqueness of $\mathbf{X}$ and $\mathbf{Y}$ experimentally by assessing solutions from multiple runs, making sure that factor matrices corresponding to the minimum function values are the same (visually).

In this study, two types of models are used: The one that is defined by the optimization problem (1) using different loss-functions $\mathcal{L}_j$, and a second one, a naïve counterpart, that uses the same constraints and regularization, but only uses a quadratic loss function across all feature columns. Hence, the second type is nonnegative matrix factorization with additional ℓ_1 regularization considered as the naive counterpart of the GLRM. In the following, we use the abbreviation GLRM to refer to the tailored model with statistical data-type-dependent loss functions, and NMF to a nonnegatiive matrix factorization model with ℓ_1 regularization. We explored different regularization parameters for the sparsity regularization, i.e., $\lambda_r, \lambda_c \in \{0.1, 1, 5, 10\}$, and observed that $\lambda_r = \lambda_c = 1$ yields sparse and significant phenotypes. Increasing the regularization parameters further yielded phenotypes that were sparser but with fewer significant subgroups.

3.2   Model Selection

One way to determine the appropriate number of components for each model is to use the imputation error. Furthermore, the imputation error allows us to compare different models [8]. For each $k-$rank model for $k \in \{1, \ldots, 16\}$, 25 different sets of held-out values are sampled. By computing corresponding GLRM and NMF models for each of the $\{\, \mathbf{Q}_i^{\mathrm{miss}} \,\}_{i=1}^{25}$, held-out values are estimated, and reconstruction error statistics are computed. We use 15% missing values for each $\mathbf{Q}_i^{\mathrm{miss}}$. Both the median of the imputation error, as well as the whole spread need to be taken into consideration. These statistics show the generalization performance and can be used to select a model. Refer to [8] for more information about how to compute imputation errors for mixed statistical data types.

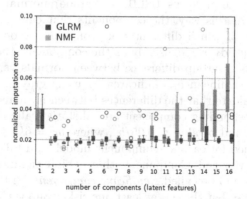

Fig. 1. Imputation error statistics for $k \in \{1, \ldots, 16\}$. The imputation error is mean-normalized within each feature and by the number of held-out values.

Prior to building the final models, outliers are removed via the leverage score [24] given by $\mathbf{h} = \mathrm{diag}(\mathbf{X} \left(\mathbf{X}^\top \mathbf{X}\right)^{-1} \mathbf{X}^\top)$, using the corresponding score matrices from the best-performing models in terms of the imputation error. Data points with a leverage score above the 99% quantile were removed (less than 50 subjects for both NMF and GLRM). The model selection process was repeated after the outliers were discarded.

3.3   General Cervical Cancer Risk Factors

For a first exploratory analysis, we investigate the imputation errors of GLRM and NMF in order to perform the model selection procedure described above. Figure 1 shows the imputation errors for $k \in \{1, \ldots, 16\}$. NMF models outperform GLRM for $k \in \{1, \ldots, 9\}$. After this range, the imputation error of NMF has high variation while GLRM is stable. In the range $k \in \{2, \ldots, 9\}$, the imputation error for both NMF and GLRM does not change much. We pick $k = 4$ since both models achieve almost the smallest error for this rank. For a 4-component model, GLRM and NMF are close with respect to their imputation error, and there are some similarities in their latent features.

Figure 2 shows the corresponding score matrices $\mathbf{X}_{nmf}$ and $\mathbf{X}_{glrm}$, as well as the features matrices $\mathbf{Y}_{nmf}$ and $\mathbf{Y}_{glrm}$ for a 4-component model. The scores are arranged according to the risk groups which is indicated by colors (green for normal, yellow for low-grade, red for high-grade, gray for cancer). Furthermore, the higher-risk groups in the figures are over-represented (cf. Table 1, Appendix) in order to compensate for the skewness of the risk-group distribution. The horizontal line within each risk group shows the mean.

Interested in whether there is a difference between different diagnosis groups, especially between normals and low-grade/high-grade risk groups, we perform unpaired t-tests for each risk group within each component. This means that, for instance, for the first component, we perform a t-test between normals vs. ASCUS low-grade, normals vs. LSLIL (low-grade), normals vs. ASC-H (high-grade), and so on. In this way, the components that capture meaningful subgroups on the basis of which different risk groups might be separated can be determined. In this study, we focus only on the components that show statistical significance in terms of group difference between normals vs. all other groups. In Fig. 2 statistical significance is indicated by using gray or blue colored bars for $\mathbf{Y}$. Blue bars indicate that the differences between normals and all other risk groups for the corresponding component are all statistically significant, i.e., for all six t-tests, we found p-value $\leq 0.05/b_k$, where $b_k = 6k$ is a Bonferroni correction that is applied for each $k-$component model, and takes into account all significance tests performed. Components that exhibit significant differences for each of the six tests will be called *significant components* in the following. Gray bars in Fig. 2 indicate that there is at least one risk-group within one component with non-significant result.

There are phenotypes that reflect higher-risk groups. Consider, for instance, the fourth component of the GLRM model, c_4^{glrm}: There are recognizably lower values for the normal diagnosis group (green) compared with higher risk groups (yellow, red, gray). The phenotype is mostly characterized by hormonal contraception usage, which is known to be a risk factor. Thus, it can be assumed that this component models a *general risk group*. This means that the latent

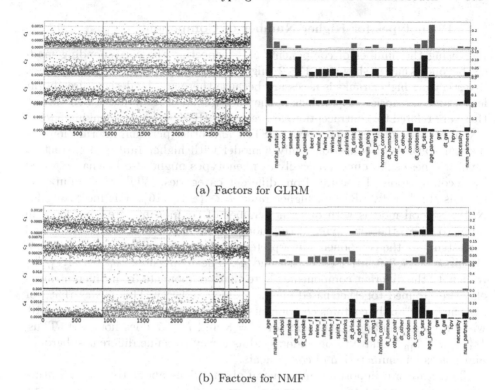

(a) Factors for GLRM

(b) Factors for NMF

Fig. 2. Left side of each plot shows a subsample of $\mathbf{X}_{nmf}$ and $\mathbf{X}_{glrm}$, respectively. The right side shows the latent features, $\mathbf{Y}_{nmf}$ and $\mathbf{Y}_{glrm}$. All factor matrices $\mathbf{X}$, $\mathbf{Y}$ are normalized by the norm of their columns and rows, respectively. $c_1, \ldots, c_4$ denote components. Colors indicate corresponding diagnosis groups: green: normal, yellow: low risk, red: high-risk, gray: cancer. Blue bars for $\mathbf{Y}_{nmf}$ and $\mathbf{Y}_{glrm}$ indicate that the differences between normals and all other risk groups are significant while gray bars indicate that there is at least one subgroup that is non-significant. See Table 3 for a description of the features. (Color figure online)

feature space hints to risk factors. For each GLRM component, there exits one (arguably sufficiently similar) corresponding NMF component. For instance, c_1^{glrm} corresponds to c_1^{nmf}, and shows a phenotype mainly defined by the features age_partner and age. For GLRM, the hormonal contraception subgroup (c_4^{glrm}) shows significance between all pairwise t-tests, while this is not the case for the corresponding NMF subgroup. Summarizing, GLRM uncovers one more significant subgroup than NMF. Maybe surprisingly, a simple NMF model together with ℓ_1 regularization can find very similar subgroups.

3.4   Phenotypes for Higher Number of Components

Increasing the number of components and inspecting the corresponding models beyond what is shown in Fig. 2 might reveal other subgroups of interest. Investigating higher ranks is necessary because there are, by design, already (at least) nine categories of questions in the questionnaire. As we described earlier, these are related to: contraception, awareness of HPV, smoking, drinking habits, sexual activity, pregnancies, previous STDs and other personal information like marital status and education. Only a model with higher rank can extract or separate these subgroups, especially as phenotypes might also be characterized by a combination of features from different categories. While the imputation error is stable for GLRM for higher ranks $k \in \{8, \ldots, 16\}$, it is increasing for NMF. Several models with different number of components are considered in order to assess the sensitivity of the model to the number of components, and consistency of the components interpreted as phenotypes. We inspect the models for $k \in \{7, 8, 9, 10\}$ (see Figs. 3 and 4). The figure uses $\{c_1^{\text{glrm}}, \ldots, c_{10}^{\text{glrm}}\}$ to denote the different components. Note that components from different models were grouped together based on the cosine similarity. This means that, for instance, c_3^{glrm} only contains components from a model with $k = 9$ and $k = 10$, while a corresponding component for $k = 8$ and $k = 7$ does not exist. Thus, $\{c_1^{\text{glrm}}, \ldots, c_{10}^{\text{glrm}}\}$ have to be understood as a way to name different subgroups and not as an enumeration of components.

There are two important and general observations about the latent feature space. First, some related features are also grouped together within components. Features that are most distinct in components c_7^{glrm}, for instance, are related to sexual habits. Second, there are many components that are consistent across models with different number of components. We say that two or more components from different $k-$component models are consistent with respect to some subgroup if there is a consensus between their most important feature weights. In some cases, phenotypes are characterized by very few prevalent features that are related, e.g., the hormonal contraception/condom subgroup c_9^{glrm}. An example for a phenotype that is consistent for all four models, is the age-partner + age (c_4^{glrm}). We use the label *complex phenotype* to denote a subgroup that is characterized by features from more than two categories.

Besides showing the phenotypes, Figs. 3 and 4 also display the Bonferroni-adjusted statistically significant subgroups (i.e., $p \leq 0.05/b_k$). Within each component, we indicate statistical significance by using either filled or unfilled bars: If every risk-group (from low-risk to cancer) deviates significantly from the normal group, the corresponding bars are colored, otherwise only the edges are shown.

Components that are consistently visible for different number of components, k, and have statistically significant deviations between normals and every other risk-groups provide strong evidence for a meaningful phenotype within the questionnaire data. Important phenotypes uncovered by GLRM are for instance c_9^{glrm} (hormonal contraception, condom, number of partners) or c_4^{glrm} (age of first sexual partner + age). Figure 4 shows the phenotypes for NMF.

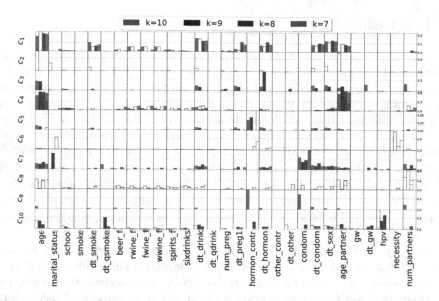

Fig. 3. Normalized $\mathbf{Y}_{\mathrm{glrm}}$ components $\{c_1^{\mathrm{glrm}}, \ldots, c_{10}^{\mathrm{glrm}}\}$ for models with $k \in \{7, 8, 9, 10\}$. Different colored bars indicate factors from the different models. Filled bars correspond to significance between all risk-levels for a certain subgroup

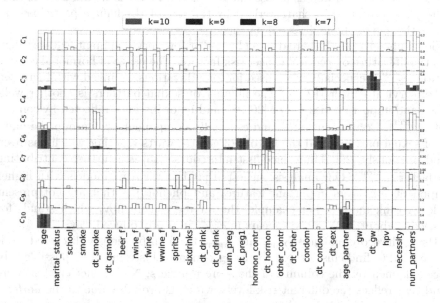

Fig. 4. Normalized $\mathbf{Y}_{\mathrm{nmf}}$ components $\{c_1^{\mathrm{nmf}}, \ldots, c_{10}^{\mathrm{nmf}}\}$ for models with $k \in \{7, 8, 9, 10\}$.

4   Discussion

For a 4-component model, NMF and GLRM both uncover phenotypes related to hormonal contraception, age + age of first sexual partner, and a complex phenotype that has a similar profile (with the exception of num_partners). The subsequent analysis using higher-rank models with $k \in \{7, 8, 9, 10\}$ suggests that using loss functions that match the data type are better suited for phenotype discovery than using standard quadratic loss functions. GLRM uncovers more phenotypes compared to NMF. Furthermore, we observe that component c_9^{glrm} shows that GLRM is able to reveal a significant subgroup that is mainly defined by two binary variables: hormon_contr and condom. Some components show that relating features are grouped together within components, e.g., c_3^{glrm} (contraception + sexual habits) or c_9^{glrm} (hormonal contraception, condom, number of partners).

Grouping of related features, consistency between different k-rank models, expert knowledge and significance between risk-levels provide evidence that (generalized) low-rank models can uncover important phenotypes. By design, the questionnaire mainly contains items that are known to be important risk factors. However, the results in this study show that significant components or subgroups that are defined by multivariate features exist. A subgroup that is found by both GLRM and NMF, as well as across different k-rank models within both models is the phenotype that is characterized by the age of the female participant as well as the age of the first sexual partner.

Some phenotypes that are defined by one or few very dominant features align with the literature on cervical cancer risk factors. The usage of hormonal contraception (c_5^{glrm}), especially when used for long durations, is linked with increased risk of cervical cancer [12,25]. The number of sexual partners is another well-known and important risk factor [26–28], and is for instance reflected by component (c_9^{glrm}). Component c_3^{glrm} and especially component c_3^{nmf} group the number of sexual partners and the history of genital warts together which has been found previously [29]. Time since first intercourse [15] is a further contributing risk factor (c_9^{glrm}). Our analysis suggests that investigating models with higher components uncovers important features and phenotypes that are not present for lower-rank models. For example, the binary feature hpv, which stands for knowledge about HPV, only appears in c_{10}^{glrm} in a pronounced way.

Using the score matrices $\mathbf{X}_{nmf}$ and $\mathbf{X}_{glrm}$ from all previously discussed models, we tried to find clusters, e.g., by using k-means clustering of all possible subspaces, defined by the columns of the score matrices. No distinct clusters were found that reflect the different risk-levels, which is probably due to the *uniform effect*: k-means clusters tend to have uniform sizes and hence cannot capture imbalanced risk-levels [30]. We assume that it is not possible to find distinct, non-overlapping clusters just based on questionnaire data, as the within-risk-level variation is too large. However, our results indicate that it is possible to uncover certain tendencies of risk-level groups.

5   Future Work

Validating phenotypes based on unpaired t-tests between risk-level groups is a limitation as differences in the means might constitute a necessary but not sufficient condition for the clinical meaningfulness of a phenotype. Testing the validity of phenotypes, i.e., their significance in a clinical context, is a challenge that might be adequately addressed by methods from *survival analysis* [1,31]. In survival analysis, the *time until an event ('hazard') occurs* is studied. In our context, this time span could be defined as the time between the completion of the questionnaire and a high-grade risk result. Different phenotypes can be evaluated with respect to their hazard times which in turn can serve as a proxy to evaluate clinical significance. Figure 5 depicts an exemplary pipeline that uses a low-rank model to compute (sparse) phenotypes that are then examined by survival analysis. Such a pipeline could uncover the important phenotypes and questions and could be beneficial for personalizing cervical cancer screening programs, in order to find a better balance between too infrequent screening and over-screening.

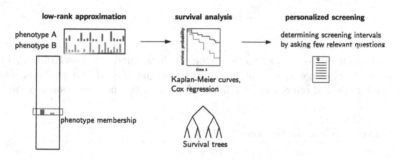

Fig. 5. Pipeline from a low-rank model to personalized screening.

6   Conclusion

In this study, (generalized) low-rank models were used for computational phenotype discovery in questionnaires that were sent out to gather meta data within the Norwegian cervical cancer screening programme. We used two decomposition methods, one that is agnostic to different data types and one that considers the different statistical data types via appropriate loss functions. Our results indicate that the careful construction of models that were tailored to the data types was worthwhile and revealed more significant phenotypes compared to the naïve counterpart. Discovering clinically-meaningful phenotypes helps to identify risk groups that are characterized by a combination of features. Phenotypes in the Norwegian questionnaire data related to the age of the first sexual partner, hormonal contraception, number of sexual partners and contraception usage, among others were identified.

Acknowledgement. This work is part of the *DeCipher* project that is funded by the Research Council of Norway.

Appendix

Table 1. Cervical cancer risk levels (cytology). The count column indicates the number of women in the corresponding risk-level group in the final data matrix. Diagnoses AGUS and ACIS are in the same high-grade(2) risk-level group.

Risk level	Description	Count
normal	no atypical cells	2346
low-grade(1)	atypical squamous cell of undetermined significance (ASCUS)	2025
low-grade(2)	low grade squamous intraepithelial lesion (LSIL)	1462
high-grade(1)	atypical squamous cells high (ASC-H)	159
high-grade(2)	atypical glandular cell of unknown significance (AGUS)	} 62
high-grade(2)	atypical endocervical cells, probably adenocarcinoma in situ (ACIS)	
high-grade(3)	high grade squamous intraepithelial lesion (HSIL)	219
cancer	-	86

Table 2. The four different loss functions (logistic loss, quadratic loss Kullback-Leibler divergence, ordinal hinge loss) that are used in posing the GLRM problem. For the ordinal loss function, d refers to the number of options for the corresponding question.

Type	Element-wise loss function
binary	$\mathcal{L}_{\log}(q, u) = \log(1 + \exp(qu))$
count	$\mathcal{L}_{\mathrm{KL}}(q, u) = u - q\log u + q\log q - q, \quad q \in \mathbb{N}, u \geq 0$
ordinal	$\mathcal{L}_{\mathrm{ord}}(q, u) = \sum_{q'=1}^{q-1}(1 - u + q')_+ + \sum_{q'=q+1}^{d}(1 + u - q')_+$
real	$\mathcal{L}_{\mathrm{quad}}(q, u) = ||q - u||_2^2$

Table 3. Summary of included features from the questionnaire, grouped by their statistical data type. Abbreviations used within this table; w: week, m: month, CCS: cervical cancer screening. For delta-time features (dt_), t stands for 'time since'.

Variable name	Meaning	Domain
— binary —		
smoke	Has smoked before	true, false
hormon_contr	Has used hormonal contraception	true, false
other_contr	Has used other hormonal contraception	true, false
condom	Has used a condom	true, false
marital_status	Is or was married	true, false
gw	Had genital warts	true, false
hpv	Has heard of HPV before	true, false
necessity	Thinks CCS is necessary	true, false
— ordinal —		
school	Years of schooling	< 12 y, 13-16 y, > 16 y
beer_f	frequency of beer consumption.	never, < 1/m, 1-3/m, 1-2/w, 3-6/w, everyday
rwine_f	frequency of red wine consumption.	
wwine_f	frequency of white wine consumption.	
fwine_f	frequency of fortified wine consumption.	
spirits_f	frequency of spirits consumption.	
sixdrinks	frequency of binge drinking	never, <1/m, 1-3/m, 4-8/m, >8/m
— real —		
age	Age of the woman	years
age_partner	Partner's age 1st intercourse	years
dt_sex	t first intercourse	years
dt_condom	t first condom usage	years
dt_hormon	t first horm. contr.	years
dt_other	t first other horm. contr.	years
dt_gw	t genital warts diagnosis	years
dt_smoke	t smoking start	years
dt_qsmoke	t smoking cessation	years
dt_drink	t drinking start	years
dt_qdrink	t drinking cessation	years
dt_preg1	t first pregnancy	years
— count —		
num_partners	Number of sexual partners	N
num_preg	Number of pregnancies	N

References

1. Perros, I., Papalexakis, E.E., Vuduc, R., Searles, E., Sun, J.: Temporal phenotyping of medically complex children via PARAFAC2 tensor factorization. J. Biomed. Inform. **93**, 103125 (2019)
2. Joshi, S., Gunasekar, S., Sontag, D., Joydeep, G.: Identifiable phenotyping using constrained non-negative matrix factorization. In: Machine Learning for Healthcare Conference, pp. 17–41. PMLR (2016)
3. Banda, J.M., Seneviratne, M., Hernandez-Boussard, T., Shah, N.H.: Advances in electronic phenotyping: from rule-based definitions to machine learning models. Annu. Rev. Biomed. Data Sci. **1**, 53–68 (2018)
4. Pearson, K.: On lines and planes of closest fit to systems of points in space. Lond. Edinb. Dublin Philos. Mag. J. Sci. **2**(11), 559–572 (1901)
5. Hotelling, H.: Analysis of a complex of statistical variables into principal components. J. Educ. Psychol. **24**(6), 417 (1933)
6. Lee, D.D., Seung, H.S.: Learning the parts of objects by non-negative matrix factorization. Nature **401**(6755), 788–791 (1999)
7. Schuler, A., et al.: Discovering patient phenotypes using generalized low rank models. In: Biocomputing 2016: Proceedings of the Pacific Symposium, pp. 144–155. World Scientific (2016)
8. Udell, M., Horn, C., Zadeh, R., Boyd, S.: Generalized low rank models. Found. Trends® Mach. Learn. **9**(1), 1–118 (2016)
9. Nygård, J., Skare, G., Thoresen, S.: The cervical cancer screening programme in Norway, 1992–2000: changes in pap smear coverage and incidence of cervical cancer. J. Med. Screen. **9**(2), 86–91 (2002)
10. Hansen, B.T., Campbell, S., Nygård, M.: Regional differences in cervical cancer incidence and associated risk behaviors among Norwegian women: a population-based study. BMC Cancer **21**(1), 1–10 (2021)
11. Hansen, B.T., Hukkelberg, S.S., Haldorsen, T., Eriksen, T., Skare, G.B., Nygård, M.: Factors associated with non-attendance, opportunistic attendance and reminded attendance to cervical screening in an organized screening program: a cross-sectional study of 12,058 Norwegian women. BMC Public Health **11**(1), 1–13 (2011)
12. Smith, J.S., et al.: Cervical cancer and use of hormonal contraceptives: a systematic review. Lancet **361**(9364), 1159–1167 (2003)
13. Sharma, P., Pattanshetty, S.M.: A study on risk factors of cervical cancer among patients attending a tertiary care hospital: a case-control study. Clin. Epidemiology Glob. Health **6**(2), 83–87 (2018)
14. Louie, K., et al.: Early age at first sexual intercourse and early pregnancy are risk factors for cervical cancer in developing countries. Br. J. Cancer **100**(7), 1191–1197 (2009)
15. Plummer, M., Peto, J., Franceschi, S., of Epidemiological studies of cervical cancer, I.C.: time since first sexual intercourse and the risk of cervical cancer. Int. J. Cancer **130**(11), 2638–2644 (2012)
16. Winkelstein JR, W.: Smoking and cervical cancer-current status: a review. Am. J. Epidemiol. **131**(6), 945–957 (1990)
17. Torres-Poveda, K., Ruiz-Fraga, I., Madrid-Marina, V., Chavez, M., Richardson, V.: High risk HPV infection prevalence and associated cofactors: a population-based study in female ISSSTE beneficiaries attending the HPV screening and early detection of cervical cancer program. BMC Cancer **19**(1), 1–12 (2019)

18. Ho, J.C., et al.: Limestone: high-throughput candidate phenotype generation via tensor factorization. J. Biomed. Inform. **52**, 199–211 (2014)
19. Ho, J.C., Ghosh, J., Sun, J.: Marble: high-throughput phenotyping from electronic health records via sparse nonnegative tensor factorization. In: KDD 2014: Proceedings of the 20th ACM SIGKDD International Conference on Knowledge Discovery and Data Mining, pp. 115–124 (2014)
20. Papalexakis, E.E., Sidiropoulos, N.D., Bro, R.: From k-means to higher-way coclustering: multilinear decomposition with sparse latent factors. IEEE Trans. Signal Process. **61**(2), 493–506 (2012)
21. Bro, R., Papalexakis, E.E., Acar, E., Sidiropoulos, N.D.: Coclustering-a useful tool for chemometrics. J. Chemom. **26**(6), 256–263 (2012)
22. Srebro, N., Jaakkola, T.: Weighted low-rank approximations. In: ICML 2003: Proceedings of the 20th International Conference on Machine Learning, pp. 720–727 (2003)
23. Collins, M., Dasgupta, S., Schapire, R.E.: A generalization of principal component analysis to the exponential family. In: Proceedings of the 14th International Conference on Neural Information Processing Systems: Natural and Synthetic, NIPS 2001, pp. 617–624. MIT Press (2001)
24. Bro, R.: PARAFAC. Tutorial and applications. Chemom. Intell. Lab. Syst. **38**(2), 149–171 (1997)
25. Cibula, D., et al.: Hormonal contraception and risk of cancer. Hum. Reprod. Update **16**(6), 631–650 (2010)
26. Liu, Z.C., Liu, W.D., Liu, Y.H., Ye, X.H., Chen, S.D.: Multiple sexual partners as a potential independent risk factor for cervical cancer: a meta-analysis of epidemiological studies. Asian Pac. J. Cancer Prev. **16**(9), 3893–3900 (2015)
27. Jensen, K.E., et al.: Women's sexual behavior. population-based study among 65 000 women from four nordic countries before introduction of human papillomavirus vaccination. Acta Obstetricia et Gynecologica Scandinavica **90**(5), 459–467 (2011)
28. Hansen, B.T., et al.: Age at first intercourse, number of partners and sexually transmitted infection prevalence among Danish, Norwegian and Swedish women: estimates and trends from nationally representative cross-sectional surveys of more than 100 000 women. Acta Obstet. Gynecol. Scand. **99**(2), 175–185 (2020)
29. Kjær, S.K., et al.: The burden of genital warts: a study of nearly 70,000 women from the general female population in the 4 Nordic countries. J. Infect. Dis. **196**(10), 1447–1454 (2007)
30. Xiong, H., Wu, J., Chen, J.: K-means clustering versus validation measures: a data-distribution perspective. IEEE Trans. Syst. Man Cybern. Part B (Cybern.) **39**(2), 318–331 (2008)
31. Bewick, V., Cheek, L., Ball, J.: Statistics review 12: survival analysis. Crit. Care **8**(5), 1–6 (2004)

Automatic Unsupervised Clustering of Videos of the Intracytoplasmic Sperm Injection (ICSI) Procedure

Andrea M. Storås[1,2](✉)[iD], Michael A. Riegler[1][iD], Trine B. Haugen[3][iD],
Vajira Thambawita[1][iD], Steven A. Hicks[1,2][iD], Hugo L. Hammer[1,2][iD],
Radhika Kakulavarapu[3][iD], Pål Halvorsen[1,2][iD], and Mette H. Stensen[4][iD]

[1] Department of Holistic Systems, Simula Metropolitan Center for Digital
Engineering, Oslo, Norway
andrea@simula.no
[2] Department of Computer Science, Faculty of Technology, Art and Design,
OsloMet - Oslo Metropolitan University, Oslo, Norway
[3] Department of Life Sciences and Health, Faculty of Health Sciences,
OsloMet - Oslo Metropolitan University, Oslo, Norway
[4] Fertilitetssenteret, Oslo, Norway

Abstract. The *in vitro* fertilization procedure called intracytoplasmic sperm injection can be used to help fertilize an egg by injecting a single sperm cell directly into the cytoplasm of the egg. In order to evaluate, refine and improve the method in the fertility clinic, the procedure is usually observed at the clinic. Alternatively, a video of the procedure can be examined and labeled in a time-consuming process. To reduce the time required for the assessment, we propose an unsupervised method that automatically clusters video frames of the intracytoplasmic sperm injection procedure. Deep features are extracted from the video frames and form the basis for a clustering method. The method provides meaningful clusters representing different stages of the intracytoplasmic sperm injection procedure. The clusters can lead to more efficient examinations and possible new insights that can improve clinical practice. Further on, it may also contribute to improved clinical outcomes due to increased understanding about the technical aspects and better results of the procedure. Despite promising results, the proposed method can be further improved by increasing the amount of data and exploring other types of features.

Keywords: Unsupervised learning · Clustering · Human reproduction · Medical videos · Computer vision

1 Introduction

Infertility is defined as a disease where an individual or a couple does not succeed in becoming clinically pregnant after a period of twelve months with regular,

E. Zouganeli et al. (Eds.): NAIS 2022, CCIS 1650, pp. 111–121, 2022.
https://doi.org/10.1007/978-3-031-17030-0_9

unprotected sexual intercourse [22]. Estimates suggest that about 190 million people worldwide are affected by infertility [9]. Assisted reproductive technology (ART) is used to treat infertility, and *in vitro* fertilization has been used for more than 40 years. The procedure called intracytoplasmic sperm injection (ICSI) [16] was introduced in the beginning of the 1990s, as a treatment for male factor infertility due to poor semen quality. Using this treatment, a single sperm is injected into the egg. The use of ICSI has greatly increased over the past years [1,7].

Visual examinations of the ICSI procedure are performed to evaluate technical aspects of the procedure. Some of the critical steps during the procedure are the selection of which sperm to inject, how the immobilization of sperm is performed, the technique used for injecting the sperm into the egg and the quality of the egg. Figures 1a to 1d illustrate different stages of the procedure, as well as debris. All video frames in the figures are from the data applied in the present study. Differences in results reported after ICSI treatments are partly explained by the level of experience of the embryologist performing the procedure, but technical variations might also be important [17]. For example, videos of the ICSI procedure can be applied for training purposes and refinement of internal procedures at the fertility clinic. Detailed understanding and control of the technical procedure may lead to improved clinical outcomes as well, such as higher fertilization and pregnancy rates. However, the examination and labeling of videos are time-consuming, and it requires knowledge about the critical steps during the procedure. Furthermore, medical professionals with such knowledge are not always available for labeling medical data, which complicates the process of obtaining labeled videos of high quality. Consequently, unsupervised learning is an attractive alternative, as it allows for training artificial intelligence (AI) models without labeled data. Because the outputs from the unsupervised models are not assigned distinct labels, some type of human interpretation of the results is required, but this still requires less work than manually labeling all samples in a dataset.

In this work, we present an unsupervised clustering technique that is able to cluster video frames from the ICSI procedure into groups that represent different stages of the procedure. This can make the examination of the videos more effective, and the health personnel will save time as they can watch the critical steps directly. Further on, focusing on the relevant parts of the procedure might contribute to easier detection of possible improvements, which could lead to improved clinical outcomes. Unsupervised clustering techniques have been developed for summarization of capsule endoscopy videos [8], detection of anomalies in computed tomography (CT) scans [3], segmentation of 3D medical images [14] and to diagnose coronavirus disease (CoVID19) from medical images [13]. None of these studies apply the same clustering algorithms as in the present paper, and they do not investigate data from the field of human reproduction. Regarding the use of AI to analyze videos of the ICSI procedure, one study trained a U-Net neural network to extract video frames of the oolemma, i.e., the cell membrane of the egg, during sperm injection [10]. To our knowledge,

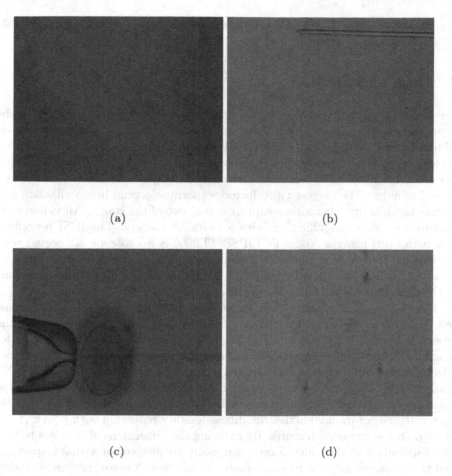

Fig. 1. Examples of video frames representing sperm selection (a), sperm immobilization (b), sperm injection (c) and debris (d). The frames arrive from the data applied in the presented work.

this is the first time unsupervised clustering has been applied to video frames of the ICSI procedure. Thus, the main contributions of this work are:

- Exploration of unsupervised learning and clustering on extracted video frames of the ICSI procedure as a tool for embryologists.
- Automatic detection of important stages in recordings of the procedure.
- Testing of the clustering method with embryologists to evaluate clinical practicability.
- The source code is provided for the implemented methodology.

In the following, Sect. 2 provides an overview of the data and methods used in this work. This is followed by a description of our experiments and a presentation of our results in Sect. 3. Next, our findings and their implications on the clinical practice are discussed in Sect. 4. Finally, we provide a conclusion and possible future directions in Sect. 5.

2   Data and Method

Seven videos of artificial reproduction using the ICSI procedure are used in the experiments. The videos arrive from a pilot study that was conducted at Fertilitetssenteret in Oslo, Norway in 2021. Because the data is anonymized, no ethical approvals are required. The resolution is 1920×1080, and the frame rate per second is 25 for all videos. The video length ranges from 15 seconds to more than 2 minutes. The longest video includes sperm selection, immobilization and injection, while the other videos capture one or two of the stages. All videos were captured at 200× magnification with a DeltaPix camera. The ICSI procedure was performed using a Nikon ECLIPSE TE2000-S microscope connected with Eppendorf TransferMan 4m micromanipulator. The sperm cells were immobilized in 5 μl Polyvinylpyrrolidone (PVP; CooperSurgical). The clinical outcome of the procedures is not included in the analysis.

Figure 2 provides an overview of the proposed workflow for unsupervised clustering. Video frames are extracted every second from the seven videos using the OpenCV library in Python [2]. The frequency of one second is chosen in order to extract frames reflecting the video contents without losing much information. The extracted frames are passed through a convolutional neural network (CNN), ResNet50 [6], that has been pre-trained on the ImageNet data set [20]. Features are extracted from the layer preceding the output layer, resulting in $2,048$ deep features per frame. Further on, dimensionality reduction with t-SNE [11] is applied on the extracted features. By reducing the dimensions of the data to two, the distribution of the video frames can easily be plotted for visual inspection, and the proposed method becomes more transparent. Moreover, dimensionality reduction has been applied prior to clustering of video frames to speed up the analysis [8]. t-SNE is chosen because it is an efficient technique for dimensionality reduction that has shown good performance on high-dimensional data points such as images [11]. When applying t-SNE, the user must specify the perplexity hyperparameter value, which can be thought of as a measure of the effective number of neighbors for each data point. Usually, the value should lie between 5 and 50 [11]. The perplexity values of 10, 15, 20 and 30 are tested for our data. The perplexity values chosen are based on the size of our dataset. The value should be smaller than the total number of samples to avoid one large cluster. On the other hand, values that are too small will result in local variations. The dimensionality reduction is evaluated by visually inspecting plots of the results, and identifying the plot with the most distinct clusters. The output from t-SNE is clustered using unsupervised clustering. Because the optimal number of clusters is not known, X-means clustering [19] is applied to determine the appropriate number of clusters. G-means clustering [5] is also tested. Both algorithms identify the optimal number of clusters in the provided data. They are wrappers around the k-means algorithm [12], and the final clusters depend on

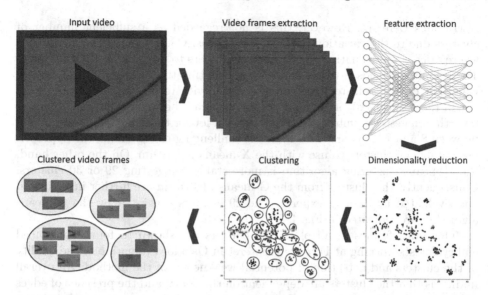

Fig. 2. The workflow for the proposed clustering method. First, video frames are extracted from videos of the ICSI procedure. The frames are then passed through a pretrained ResNet50 for extraction of deep features. The dimensionality is reduced using t-SNE before the frames are clustered using either X-means or G-means.

the cluster initialization. Consequently, the results can vary between runs even though the dataset is the same. While X-means applies the Bayesian Information Criterion to find the appropriate cluster number, G-means, on the other hand, uses a Gaussian fit. The G-means algorithm has shown higher performance than X-means when the clusters are non-spherical [5]. All code is written in Python. Pyclustering is applied for unsupervised clustering [15], and Pytorch [18] is used for extracting the deep features from the pretrained ResNet50 model [6]. The source code is publicly available online[1].

The quality of the clustering is evaluated by experienced embryologists working at Fertilitetssenteret in Oslo, Norway. The clusters are also categorized into which stage of the ICSI procedure they represent to evaluate the accuracy of the methods, but this is regarded as less important than the feedback from the embryologists.

3   Results

In total, 359 images are extracted from the seven videos. The extracted deep features are reduced to two dimensions using t-SNE. Following visual inspection, the best perplexity hyperparameter value for t-SNE is 20, leading to the most distinct clusters. The results are shown in Fig. 3. Regarding the unsupervised clustering, the X-means algorithm suggested two clusters for the data when no

---

[1] https://github.com/AndreaStoraas/UnsupervisedClustering_ICSI.

restrictions were set. However, this is not regarded as a sufficient number of clusters due to the variation between the frames. Consequently, the algorithms are restricted to estimating the number of clusters to lie between eight and 200. These limits are chosen to get clusters representing the variation in the dataset while not creating clusters that are too small with respect to the dataset size. When the X-means algorithm is forced to generate between eight and 200 clusters, the suggested number of clusters varies a lot for the same data set, ranging between 8 and 15 clusters. This makes it challenging to determine the appropriate number of clusters to use with the X-means algorithm. On the other hand, the G-means clustering algorithm is more stable, suggesting 29 or 30 clusters. Consequently, the clusters from the G-means algorithm are further investigated and evaluated by domain experts. The 29 clusters suggested by the G-means algorithm are indicated in Fig. 4.

The video frames in all of the 29 clusters are shown to four experienced embryologists working at Fertilitetssenteret in Oslo for evaluation of the quality of the clusters and detection of potential weaknesses of the method. An overall finding is that the clusters are dependent on the colors and the presence of edges in the frames. Moreover, two of the experts, one being a senior embryologist and the other one being a clinical embryologist, manually categorize the clusters after examination of typical examples of video frames from different clusters. Based on their feedback, the clusters are categorized into three subgroups that represent different critical stages of the ICSI procedure: sperm selection, sperm immobilization, and sperm injection. Video frames from these three subgroups can be studied more closely to inspect which sperm was selected, how it was immobilized and the technique applied when injecting the sperm into the egg. A fourth subgroup is also created for video frames containing bubbles and debris, here defined as noise.

The feedback from the embryologists is the main evaluation of the method. However, the accuracy of the clustering was also investigated as a secondary measure of performance. Based on visual inspection, 82% of the frames are automatically assigned to a cluster belonging to the same category. The categories were provided by the domain experts, as described above. The sperm selection seems to be the easiest part of the ICSI procedure to recognize. Still, some frames representing sperm immobilization were clustered together with sperm selection frames. Figures 5a and 5b show examples of video frames that were clustered as sperm selection according to the cluster categories from the domain experts. Figure 5a agrees with the cluster category, while Fig. 5b disagrees. Sperm immobilization is most difficult to recognize by the method, as all the clusters that include frames from this part also contain frames presenting sperm injection or sperm selection. Video frames that were clustered as sperm immobilization are provided in Figs. 5 c and 5d. Figure 5c agrees with the cluster category, while Fig. 5d disagrees.

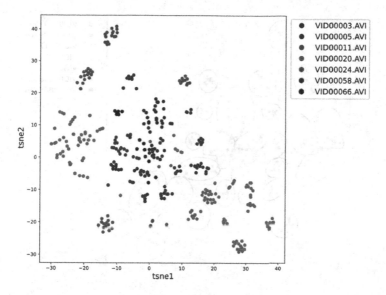

Fig. 3. Plot of the 359 images after feature extraction with a pretrained convolutional neural network and dimensionality reduction with t-SNE. The frames are colored after which video they belong to.

4   Discussion

In this work, we show that unsupervised clustering can be applied for extracting video frames from different stages of the ICSI procedure. Despite promising results, there are some limitations to be discussed. First, the proposed technique is negatively affected by the colors and edges present in the frames. Indeed, colors and edges can vary between different dishes and droplets. To make the method more robust, features that do not rely on these properties will be explored for future experiments. To reduce the variation in colors, the frames can be converted into grayscale before they are analyzed. Further on, global features such as Tamura features [21] or fuzzy color and texture histogram [4] can be applied for less dependency on the presence of edges.

Moreover, our data set included seven videos from the same fertility center. Consequently, it is not known how well they generalize to larger data sets or other clinics. Since the method is sensitive to variations in colors and edges, the performance could be affected by the resolution, light and type of camera applied during the recording of the procedure. A follow-up study is planned with more videos, as well as information about the outcome, such as fertilization status, egg degeneration rate, embryo quality, embryo development, implantation and pregnancy rates.

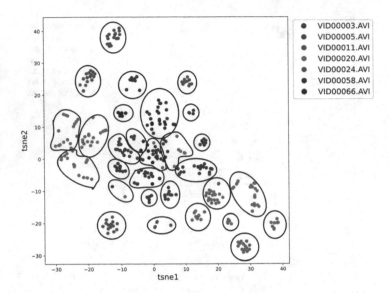

Fig. 4. Results from unsupervised clustering. The 29 clusters identified by the G-means algorithm for the 359 video frames are indicated with circles.

Our results suggest that the sperm selection stage was easiest to detect with the proposed method. The sperm selection stage does not contain any needles or eggs, which might explain why this stage is more easily separated from the other stages. The stage that was most difficult to separate was the immobilization of sperm. This could be because the sperm cells are relatively small compared to the size of the injection needle, as well as the presence of noise in the frames, making it challenging to distinguish features from these frames from features representing only noise or sperm injection.

After manual inspection of the clusters, 82% of the video frames were placed in a cluster representing the same category, as defined by domain experts. Some frames were placed in clusters representing a different category, meaning that the medical experts will encounter some frames that are not appropriate for a given stage of the ICSI procedure. Nevertheless, since most of the frames in each cluster are similar, the clusters would still be useful for a more efficient examination of the ICSI procedure. With the additional experiments suggested above, the percentage of video frames disagreeing with their cluster category might also be further reduced. Further on, the labeled clusters from our experiments can potentially be used as labels in a supervised or semi-supervised learning framework in order to categorize new video frames.

Normally, the ICSI procedure is evaluated through live observation at the clinic. Alternatively, recordings of the procedure can be watched and labeled manually. According to the senior embryologist at Fertilitetssenteret, our method proposes a more time-efficient way to improve training and quality assessment of the ICSI procedure. Because this potentially leads to improved results of the

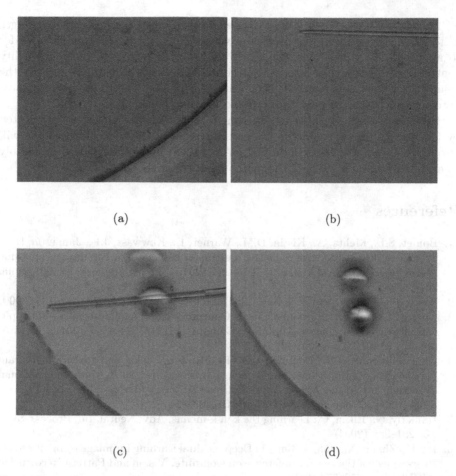

(a)   (b)

(c)   (d)

Fig. 5. Examples of video frames in clusters representing sperm selection (a, b) and sperm immobilization (c, d), according to the cluster categories provided by domain experts. Frames **a** and **c** agree with their assigned cluster labels, while **b** and **d** are video frames that were placed in clusters with a different category.

procedure, the clinical outcome, such as higher fertilization and pregnancy rates, might also improve. Finally, it could benefit couples suffering from infertility as well as the healthcare personnel performing the treatment.

5   Conclusion

In this paper, we present an unsupervised method for clustering of video frames of the popular *in vitro* fertilization technique called ICSI. Deep features are extracted from the video frames before dimensionality reduction is applied. Clustering is then performed on the resulting data points. The clusters are evaluated by experienced domain experts, and the findings are discussed. The source code for the proposed method is available online.

In conclusion, our method is able to separate video frames into different stages of the ICSI procedure. This could be valuable in the fertility clinic in order to analyze ICSI videos more efficiently for training purposes, internal quality control and refinement of internal procedures. Further on, it might improve the results after treatments with ICSI, which in turn could lead to improved clinical outcomes such as higher fertilization and pregnancy rates.

For future work, we plan to experiment with features that are less affected by the change of color and the presence of edges in the video frames. We will also use a larger data set containing an increased number of videos preferably from different clinics to see if the method can be further improved.

References

1. Boulet, S.L., Mehta, A., Kissin, D.M., Warner, L., Kawwass, J.F., Jamieson, D.J.: Trends in use of and reproductive outcomes associated with intracytoplasmic sperm injection. JAMA **313**(3), 255–263 (2015). https://doi.org/10.1001/jama. 2014.17985
2. Bradski, G.: The OpenCV library. Dr. Dobb's J. Softw. Tools **120**, 122–125 (2000)
3. Chaira, T.: A novel intuitionistic fuzzy C means clustering algorithm and its application to medical images. Appl. Soft Comput. **11**(2), 1711–1717 (2011). https:// doi.org/10.1016/j.asoc.2010.05.005
4. Chatzichristofis, S.A., Boutalis, Y.S.: FCTH: fuzzy color and texture histogram - a low level feature for accurate image retrieval. In: 2008 Ninth International Workshop on Image Analysis for Multimedia Interactive Services, pp. 191–196 (2008). https://doi.org/10.1109/WIAMIS.2008.24
5. Hamerly, G., Elkan, C.: Learning the k in k-means. Adv. Neural. Inf. Process. Syst. **16**, 281–288 (2004)
6. He, K., Zhang, X., Ren, S., Sun, J.: Deep residual learning for image recognition. In: Proceedings of the IEEE Conference on Computer Vision and Pattern Recognition (CVPR), pp. 770–778 (2016)
7. Wyns, C., et al.: ART in Europe, 2017: results generated from European registries by ESHRE. Hum. Reprod. Open **2021**(3) (2021). https://doi.org/10.1093/hropen/ hoab026
8. Iakovidis, D.K., Tsevas, S., Maroulis, D., Polydorou, A.: Unsupervised summarisation of capsule endoscopy video. In: 2008 4th International IEEE Conference Intelligent Systems, vol. 1, pp. 3-15–3-20 (2008). https://doi.org/10.1109/IS.2008. 4670414
9. Inhorn, M.C., Patrizio, P.: Infertility around the globe: new thinking on gender, reproductive technologies and global movements in the 21st century. Hum. Reprod. Update **21**(4), 411–426 (2015). https://doi.org/10.1093/humupd/dmv016
10. Jain, R., et al.: P-280 changes in oolemma height during ICSI injection on day 0 is associated with day 5–6 blastocyst formation. Hum. Reprod. **36**(Supplement_1), i263 (2021)
11. Van der Maaten, L., Hinton, G.: Visualizing data using t-SNE. J. Mach. Learn. Res. **9**(11), 2579–2605 (2008)
12. MacQueen, J., et al.: Some methods for classification and analysis of multivariate observations. In: Proceedings of the Fifth Berkeley Symposium on Mathematical Statistics and Probability, vol. 1, pp. 281–297. University of California (1967)

13. Mittal, H., Pandey, A.C., Pal, R., Tripathi, A.: A new clustering method for the diagnosis of CoVID19 using medical images. Appl. Intell. **51**(5), 2988–3011 (2021). https://doi.org/10.1007/s10489-020-02122-3

14. Moriya, T., et al.: Unsupervised segmentation of 3D medical images based on clustering and deep representation learning. In: Gimi, B., Krol, A. (eds.) Medical Imaging 2018: Biomedical Applications in Molecular, Structural, and Functional Imaging, vol. 10578, pp. 483–489. International Society for Optics and Photonics, SPIE (2018). https://doi.org/10.1117/12.2293414

15. Novikov, A.: PyClustering: data mining library. J. Open Source Softw. **4**(36), 1230 (2019). https://doi.org/10.21105/joss.01230

16. Palermo, G., Joris, H., Devroey, P., Van Steirteghem, A.: Pregnancies after intracytoplasmic injection of single spermatozoon into an oocyte. Lancet **340**(8810), 17–18 (1992). https://doi.org/10.1016/0140-6736(92)92425-F. Originally published as Volume 2, Issue 8810

17. Palermo, G.D., Neri, Q.V., Rosenwaks, Z.: To ICSI or not to ICSI. In: Seminars in Reproductive Medicine, vol. 33, pp. 92–102. Thieme Medical Publishers (2015). https://doi.org/10.1055/s-0035-1546825

18. Paszke, A., et al.: Pytorch: an imperative style, high-performance deep learning library. In: Wallach, H., Larochelle, H., Beygelzimer, A., d'Alché-Buc, F., Fox, E., Garnett, R. (eds.) Advances in Neural Information Processing Systems, vol. 32, pp. 8024–8035. Curran Associates, Inc. (2019)

19. Pelleg, D., Moore, A.W.: X-means: extending k-means with efficient estimation of the number of clusters. In: ICML, vol. 1, pp. 727–734 (2000)

20. Russakovsky, O., et al.: ImageNet large scale visual recognition challenge. Int. J. Comput. Vision **115**(3), 211–252 (2015). https://doi.org/10.1007/s11263-015-0816-y

21. Tamura, H., Mori, S., Yamawaki, T.: Textural features corresponding to visual perception. IEEE Trans. Syst. Man Cybern. **8**(6), 460–473 (1978). https://doi.org/10.1109/TSMC.1978.4309999

22. WHO: International classification of diseases, 11th revision (ICD-11) (2018). https://icd.who.int/en

Towards New AI Methods

The Kernelized Taylor Diagram

Kristoffer Wickstrøm[1]([✉])[iD], J. Emmanuel Johnson[2][iD], Sigurd Løkse[1][iD], Gustau Camps-Valls[2][iD], Karl Øyvind Mikalsen[1,4][iD], Michael Kampffmeyer[1,3][iD], and Robert Jenssen[1,3][iD]

[1] UiT the Arctic University of Norway, Tromsø, Norway
kristoffer.k.wickstrom@uit.no
[2] Universitat de València, València, Spain
[3] Norwegian Computing Center, Oslo, Norway
[4] University Hospital of North Norway, Tromsø, Norway

Abstract. This paper presents the kernelized Taylor diagram, a graphical framework for visualizing similarities between data populations. The kernelized Taylor diagram builds on the widely used Taylor diagram, which is used to visualize similarities between populations. However, the Taylor diagram has several limitations such as not capturing non-linear relationships and sensitivity to outliers. To address such limitations, we propose the kernelized Taylor diagram. Our proposed kernelized Taylor diagram is capable of visualizing similarities between populations with minimal assumptions of the data distributions. The kernelized Taylor diagram relates the maximum mean discrepancy and the kernel mean embedding in a single diagram, a construction that, to the best of our knowledge, have not been devised prior to this work. We believe that the kernelized Taylor diagram can be a valuable tool in data visualization.

Keywords: Kernel methods · Taylor diagram · Data visualization

1 Introduction

Clear and informative visualization of similarities between populations is a key component both in the development of methodology and in scientific publications. Depending on the particular use case, a wide range of techniques are available. One such visualization technique is the Taylor diagram (TD) [10], which was devised to relate several statistical quantities and allow for comparison of numerous data points in a single diagram. The TD has been frequently used in numerous application, and particularly in climate sciences [6,8]. However, the statistical quantities displayed in the TD does have some weaknesses that limit the usability of the diagram. For instance, one quantity in the diagram is the Pearson correlation coefficient, which only models linear relationship and can be sensitive to outliers. This curtails the TD, as many real-world applications use data with outliers and that are connected through non-linear relationships.

E. Zouganeli et al. (Eds.): NAIS 2022, CCIS 1650, pp. 125–131, 2022.
https://doi.org/10.1007/978-3-031-17030-0_10

One of the most well-known and widely used approaches for measuring similarity in machine learning is through kernel methods [3,4]. At its core, a kernel function corresponds to a dot product in a high-dimensional feature space, where non-linear relationship between data in the input space can be linearly related in the new feature space. As long as the kernel is positive definite, the mapping to the feature space does not have to be computed explicitly.

In this paper we propose the kernelized Taylor diagram (KTD), which is illustrated in Fig. 1. This diagram relates well-known quantities from the kernel literature [9], namely the maximum mean discrepancy (MMD) and the kernel mean embedding in a single

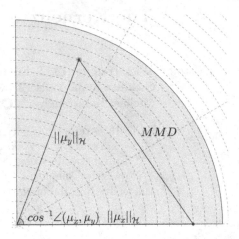

Fig. 1. KTD: The radial distance from the origin to each point is proportional to the length of kernel mean embedding. The distance between the points is the maximum mean discrepancy.

figure. To the best of our knowledge, such a diagram has never been devised prior to this work. The KTD makes no assumptions on the distributions of the populations and can model a rich family of relationships between populations. The functionality of the proposed diagram is demonstrated on synthetic data. Code: https://github.com/Wickstrom/KernelizedTaylorDiagram.

2   The Kernelized Taylor Diagram

Taylor Diagram. The TD was introduced as a tool that could relate several statistical quantities in a single figure [10]. It strength lies in the ability to compare numerous data points where it would otherwise be necessary to utilized several figures and/or tables. The theoretical starting point of the TD is the Pearson correlation coefficient ρ and the root-mean-squared-error E between two data points. [10] argued that neither are sufficient to capture potential similarities on their own, but in the aggregate the they are capable of detecting a wide range of differences between data points. Let $\mathbf{x}$ and $\mathbf{z}$ represent two D-dimensional vectors representing two data points. The correlation coefficient between $\mathbf{x}$ and $\mathbf{z}$ is defined as:

$$\rho = \frac{1}{D} \sum_{d=1}^{D} \frac{(x_d - \bar{x})(y_d - \bar{z})}{\sigma_x \sigma_y}, \tag{1}$$

where $\bar{x}$ and $\bar{y}$ are the mean values and σ_x and σ_y are the standard deviations. The root-mean-squared-error for mean centered data points is defined as:

$$E^2 = \mathbb{E}\left[\frac{1}{D}\sum_{d=1}^{D}\left((x_d - \bar{x}) - (z_d - \bar{z})\right)^2\right]$$

$$= \frac{1}{D^2}\mathbb{E}\left[\sum_{d=1}^{D}(x_d - \bar{x})^2\right] + \frac{1}{D^2}\mathbb{E}\left[\sum_{d=1}^{D}(y_d - \bar{y})^2\right] - \frac{1}{D^2}\mathbb{E}\left[\sum_{d=1}^{D}(x_d - \bar{x})(y_d - \bar{y})\right]$$

$$\underbrace{\qquad\qquad}_{\sigma_x^2} \quad \underbrace{\qquad\qquad}_{\sigma_y^2} \quad \underbrace{\qquad\qquad\qquad}_{\sigma_{xy}}$$

$$= \sigma_x^2 + \sigma_y^2 - 2\sigma_x\sigma_y\rho. \tag{2}$$

The key point of the TD is recognize the relationship between the statistical quantities in Eq. 2 and the law of cosines:

$$c^2 = a^2 + b^2 - 2ab\cos(\theta). \tag{3}$$

Here, a and b are the lengths of two sides of a triangle with angle θ between each other and an opposite side of length c. The TD has seen widespread use in several domains such as in geophysical sciences [6,8]. Nevertheless, the TD has some key weaknesses that limits it functionality in many practical applications. The Pearson correlation coefficient has a number of limitations [1]. It can only model linear relationships [2], which can be restricting in many practical application. Also, the Pearson correlation coefficient is known be sensitive to outliers [1].

The Kernelized Taylor Diagram. To address such limitations, we propose the KTD, which uses well-know measures from the kernel literature to model similarities between populations. The starting point of the KTD is one of the most widely used distance measures in the kernel literature, namely the maximum mean discrepancy (MMD) [7], which measures the distance between two distributions where each distributions is represented by a mean embedding of the data. Let $X \sim P$ and $Y \sim Q$, and $\boldsymbol{\mu}_x$ and $\boldsymbol{\mu}_y$ denoted the mean embedding vectors representing two distributions P and Q. Then, the MMD is defined as the norm between the two embeddings in a reproducing kernel Hilbert space $\mathcal{H}$:

$$\begin{aligned}
MMD^2 &= \|\boldsymbol{\mu}_x - \boldsymbol{\mu}_y\|_{\mathcal{H}}^2 \\
&= \|\boldsymbol{\mu}_x\|_{\mathcal{H}}^2 + \|\boldsymbol{\mu}_y\|_{\mathcal{H}}^2 - 2\langle\boldsymbol{\mu}_x, \boldsymbol{\mu}_y\rangle_{\mathcal{H}} \\
&= \|\boldsymbol{\mu}_x\|_{\mathcal{H}}^2 + \|\boldsymbol{\mu}_y\|_{\mathcal{H}}^2 - 2\|\boldsymbol{\mu}_x\|_{\mathcal{H}}\|\boldsymbol{\mu}_y\|_{\mathcal{H}}\frac{\langle\boldsymbol{\mu}_x, \boldsymbol{\mu}_y\rangle_{\mathcal{H}}}{\|\boldsymbol{\mu}_x\|_{\mathcal{H}}\|\boldsymbol{\mu}_y\|_{\mathcal{H}}} \\
&= \|\boldsymbol{\mu}_x\|_{\mathcal{H}}^2 + \|\boldsymbol{\mu}_y\|_{\mathcal{H}}^2 - 2\|\boldsymbol{\mu}_x\|_{\mathcal{H}}\|\boldsymbol{\mu}_y\|_{\mathcal{H}}\cos\angle(\boldsymbol{\mu}_x, \boldsymbol{\mu}_y).
\end{aligned} \tag{4}$$

In general, the true data distributions are not known, so the mean embeddings are replaced by empirical mean embeddings that are estimated based on samples from each distribution:

$$\hat{\boldsymbol{\mu}}_x = \frac{1}{N}\sum_{n=1}^{N}\kappa(\mathbf{x}_n, \cdot), \tag{5}$$

where $\kappa(\cdot, \cdot)$ is a positive definite kernel that measures similarity between data points. If the kernel is characteristic [7], MMD is a metric and is zero only if the two distributions are equal. [5] showed that the well-known Gaussian kernel with kernel width σ, $G_\sigma(\mathbf{x}_i, \mathbf{x}_j) = \exp(||\mathbf{x}_i - \mathbf{x}_j||^2/2\sigma)$, is a characteristic kernel. Furthermore, MMD does not assume a particular distribution of the data, and can capture both non-linear and linear relationships between distributions.

Similarly as with the TD, we recognize the law of cosines in Eq. 4. The mean embeddings of the two distributions are the side lengths of a triangle with angle $\cos \angle(\boldsymbol{\mu}_x, \boldsymbol{\mu}_y)$ between each other and an opposite side with length equal to the MMD between the distributions. The KTD is shown in Fig. 1.

The length of the mean embeddings indicate the distance from the origin to each point in the KTD. For the Gaussian kernel, the kernel mean embedding captures all moments of the data population [9]. But it is not obvious how to interpret what information the kernel mean embeddings are illustrating in the diagram. However, the kernel mean embeddings can be related to uncertainty through the information potential (IP) from information theoretic learning [11], which allows for a similar interpretation of the KTD as the TD. That is, the kernel mean embeddings correspond to the σ in Eq. 2. In most applications, the IP must be estimated from data. In information theoretic learning, the IP is often estimated through the quadratic IP estimator using a Gaussian kernel [11]:

$$\hat{V}_{2,\sigma}(X) = \frac{1}{N^2} \sum_{i,j}^{N} G_\sigma(\mathbf{x}_i, \mathbf{x}_j). \tag{6}$$

Next, the squared norm terms in Eq. 4 can be expressed as:

$$\|\boldsymbol{\mu}_x\|_{\mathcal{H}}^2 = \frac{1}{N^2} \sum_{i,j}^{N} \kappa(\mathbf{x}_i, \mathbf{x}_j). \tag{7}$$

If the mean embeddings are calculated using a Gaussian kernel, Eq. 6 and Eq. 7 are equivalent. Furthermore, the IP is related to entropy as follows:

$$\hat{H}_2(X) = -\log(\hat{V}_{2,\sigma}(X)). \tag{8}$$

Entropy measures the amount of information in a random variable, but can also be interpreted as a measure of uncertainty. High entropy indicates more variation in the data, while low entropy means that the data is clustered together. From Eq. 8 it is evident that when the information potential of X is high and the entropy will be low, and the opposite when the information potential of X is low. For the KTD, this means that random variables with a high value for the kernel mean embedding, and thus far from the origin, is associated with low uncertainty, and oppositely for a low value of the kernel mean embedding. This insight is important, as it allows us to relate concepts from the TD to the KTD.

3   Experiments

To illustrate the functionality of the KTD we consider the case were the true distribution of the data is known and generate 1000 samples from 5 different populations. The reference distribution X_{ref} is sampled from a standard normal distribution. The remaining populations are constructed as follows:

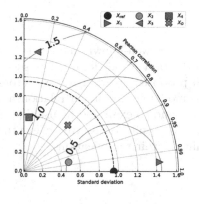 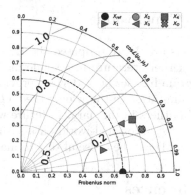

(a) Taylor diagram   (b) Kernelized Taylor diagram

Fig. 2. Comparison of TD with the KTD on the data described in Sect. 3. The experiment illustrates how the TD is not able to capture non-linear dependencies and is sensitive to outliers, when compared with the proposed KTD.

$$X_1 \sim 2X_{\text{ref}} + \epsilon, \quad X_2 \sim \frac{X_{\text{ref}}}{2} + \epsilon, X_3 \sim X_{\text{ref}}^2 + \epsilon,$$

$$X_4 \sim X_{\text{ref}}\sin(X_{\text{ref}}) + \epsilon, X_O \sim \frac{X_{\text{ref}}}{2} + \epsilon \text{ (with outliers)},$$

where $\epsilon \sim \mathcal{N}(0, 0.01)$. Population X_1 and X_2 are chosen to represent a linear relationship to the reference distribution, but with different scaling such that the standard deviation is different compared to the reference. Population X_3 and X_4 are chosen to represent a non-linear relationship with the reference. Lastly, X_O is chosen to also have a linea relationship with the reference, but with two outliers added to the population. These two outliers are samples from $\mathcal{N}(10, 1)$.

Figure 2a displays the TD for these populations in relation to the reference distribution, while Fig. 2b shows the KTD. First, we consider Fig. 2a. Note that X_1 and X_2 both have a high similarity with the reference but with different length from the origin as a result of the difference in standard deviation. Next, both X_3 and X_4 are indicated as having low similarity with the reference, which is expected since the relationship is non-linear. Lastly, X_O, which is almost identical to X_2 except for two outliers, shows a much lower similarity score. This illustrates how sensitive the TD can be to outliers.

In Fig. 2b, X_1 and X_2 also shows a related and high similarity score. However, note that compared to Fig. 2a, the distance to the origin have been changed, which is explained through the connection to the information potential described in Sect. 2. Next, both X_3 and X_4 are now indicated to have a high similarity with the reference, which illustrates that the KTD is capable of capturing non-linear similarities. Lastly, X_2 and X_O are located at almost the same point in the diagram, which shows that the KTD is robust against outliers in the data.

4   Conclusion

In this article we proposed the KTD, which relates well-known quantities from the kernel literature in a single diagram. To the best of our knowledge, such a diagram has not been devised previously. Our proposed diagram addresses some key limitation in the widely used TD, such as modeling non-linear relationships and outliers in the data. In future works, we intend to examine the usability of the diagram on real-world data such as in climate applications. We believe that the KTD can be a useful tool in many machine learning applications.

References

1. Armstrong, R.A.: Should pearson's correlation coefficient be avoided? Ophthalmic Physiol. Opt. **39**(5), 316–327 (2019)
2. Correa, C.D., Lindstrom, P.: The mutual information diagram for uncertainty visualization. Int. J. Uncertain. Quantif. **3**, 187–201 (2013)
3. Cortes, C., Mohri, M., Rostamizadeh, A.: Algorithms for learning kernels based on centered alignment. J. Mach. Learn. Res. **13**, 795–828 (2012)
4. Cristianini, N., Shawe-Taylor, J., Elisseeff, A., Kandola, J.: On kernel-target alignment. In: Neural Information Processing Systems, pp. 367–373. MIT Press (2002)
5. Fukumizu, K., Gretton, A., Sun, X., Schölkopf, B.: Kernel measures of conditional dependence. In: Neural Information Processing Systems, vol. 20 (2008)
6. Gleckler, P.J., Taylor, K.E., Doutriaux, C.: Performance metrics for climate models. J. Geophys. Res. Atmos. **113**(D6) (2008)
7. Gretton, A., Borgwardt, K.M., Rasch, M.J., Schölkopf, B., Smola, A.: A kernel two-sample test. J. Mach. Learn. Res. **13**, 723–773 (2012)
8. Jakob Themeßl, M., Gobiet, A., Leuprecht, A.: Empirical-statistical downscaling and error correction of daily precipitation from regional climate models. Int. J. Climatol. **31**(10), 1530–1544 (2011)
9. Muandet, K., Fukumizu, K., Sriperumbudur, B., Schölkopf, B.: Kernel mean embedding of distributions: a review and beyond. Founds. Trends Mach. Learn. **10**(1–2), 1–141 (2017)
10. Taylor, K.E.: Summarizing multiple aspects of model performance in a single diagram. J. Geophys. Res. Atmos. **106**(D7), 7183–7192 (2001)
11. Xu, D., Erdogmuns, D.: Renyi's entropy, divergence and their nonparametric estimators. In: Principe, J.C. (ed.) Information Theoretic Learning. ISS, pp. 47–102. Springer, New York (2010). https://doi.org/10.1007/978-1-4419-1570-2_2

Simulating University Application Data for Fair Matchings

Meirav Segal[✉], Anne-Marie George, and Christos Dimitrakakis

Department of Informatics, University of Oslo, Oslo, Norway
{meiravs,annemage,chridim}@ifi.uio.no

Abstract. This paper describes the design of a simulator (work in progress), that is based on Norwegian university admissions and exam data. It generates a realistic population of applicants to university programs, their preferences and study outcomes if they were admitted to the different study programs. This simulator is a versatile tool and can be used to analyse the current admission policy for Norwegian universities in terms of many fairness criteria that, e.g., take into account student preferences, gender balance, university preferences and study outcomes. More generally, it creates a benchmark for testing matching algorithms and fairness notions without revealing sensitive data.

1 Introduction

The problem of school choice, in which students are assigned to schools, is a popular research area lying in the intersection of computer science, economics and mathematics. Apart from being challenging, it has great importance due to the significant influence a school choice could have on students' future trajectories. Formally it constitutes a matching or allocation problem under preference in a bipartite graph. Algorithmic solutions are employed in many countries and similar areas, e.g., for university admissions in Hungary [5], allocation of teachers to positions in France [11] and patient-donor matches for kidneys in many countries [4]. These solutions often involve stable allocations based on students and schools preferences, capacities and other constraints enforcing formal requirements or some fairness towards subgroups. Here, stability means that no single deviation from the computed allocation is more beneficial for any party involved [6].

When designing new algorithms and methods for school choice problems, there is an obvious need to evaluate its performance in practice, preferably using real-world data. While stable allocations consider candidates' preferences, other methods might take into account future study outcomes such as dropouts or grades. Nevertheless, real-life data cannot provide outcomes for students that never participated in a study program. Thus, there is a need for a simulator that generates realistic application data and provides study outcomes for any possible allocation of students to study programs.

For example, a recent study evaluated how different policies affect dropouts in the Chilean centralized college admission system using a simulator based on

E. Zouganeli et al. (Eds.): NAIS 2022, CCIS 1650, pp. 132–138, 2022.
https://doi.org/10.1007/978-3-031-17030-0_11

real data [7]. As the simulator itself was not published, the research community cannot generate new samples to explore other questions.

We describe the planned design of a simulator based on data of the Norwegian university admission system. This data is not openly available because it contains sensitive information, but a simulator can provide reliable data for analysis while preserving privacy. This will constitute a valuable benchmark for the research community. The simulator will generate a set of applicants with demographic features (e.g. age, gender, county), educational background (e.g. high school points), their preferences over study programs and study outcomes for each of these programs. Using these attributes, decision makers can evaluate new policies. For example, the current admission system grants bonus points based on age and gender. Through simulation, we can compare students' outcomes according to assignments given by the current system, with outcomes according to assignments based on a new policy, with increased or decreased bonus points.

2   University Admissions in Norway

In Norway, the admission process for most undergraduate study programs at all public academic institutions is coordinated by the Norwegian Universities and Colleges Admission Service in a centralized manner [2]. This section describes the admission process and the available data for applications and study outcomes.

2.1   Admission Process

Candidates rank 10 study programs they wish to attend. Further, university programs specify their preferences over students by a point scheme based on grades and other factors such as age, gender or military service. In addition, candidates can apply through different quotas. For example, the first-time diplomas quota is designated for candidates who have completed and passed upper secondary school in normal time and are at most 21 years old. Other quotas are intended for underrepresented groups in specific programs. All candidates who do not fit special quotas, apply through the ordinary quota.[1] An applicant is classified as 'qualified' for a study program when they meet its minimum requirements.

In the main admission process, a specialized stable marriage algorithm is applied in order to find the candidate-optimal stable matching based on the applicants' and university programs' preferences [9]. At this point, each candidate is given at most one offer, to the highest ranked program that the candidate is qualified for (while maintaining stability).

After the candidates have accepted or declined the offers, study programs with remaining vacancies continue to make offers to available students over a period of one month in order of their preferences over the applicants.

---

[1] For more details of the point system and quotas see https://www.samordnaopptak. no/info/.

2.2   Data

Through the Norwegian Database for Statistics on Higher Education [1], we have been granted access to two data sets: Applications and Exams.

Applications. Application data[2] of all applications to all Norwegian university programs in the period 2017–2020. This data set includes $2,265,418$ applications of $\sim 500,000$ candidates to over $2,000$ study programs of 34 academic institutions. In each year approximately $180,000$ candidates apply, from which 50% are admitted.[3] Every application includes the following features:

- *Candidate features*: identifier, age, gender, citizenship, country of educational background, high school grades in the form of GPA and summarised language/science points, 'other points' (for other factors such as age or gender), registered municipality of residence (for applications made in 2020).
- *Program features*: identifier, department, university.
- *Application features*: year and semester of application, and quota the application is considered in.
- *Candidate preference*: Preference for the program (a number between 1–10).
- *Admission decision*: Study offer and acceptance.

Exams. Exam data[4] of all students at Norwegian universities for all their taken exams in the period 2017–2020. The exam data includes $5,321,519$ records of exams taken by students, with an average of 8 exam grades per student. For each year there are grades of approximately $30,000$ courses throughout the different study programs. More specifically, we consider the following entries:

- *Student identifier* (matched with entry in application table).
- *Program features*: identifier, department, university.
- *Exam features*: course identifier and number of credits, year and semester of exam, indication whether the student is retaking the exam.
- *Study outcome*: grade ('A'-'F' or Pass/Fail), or indication of non-attendance.

3   Simulator

In this section we describe the (planned) components of the simulator individually. Figure 1a presents the process of generating a new population given the trained components. First, we generate background attributes of candidates. In addition, we generate the candidate's underlying type. This type determines the preference profile, which together with background features sets the priorities over programs. The outcome profile and outcomes over programs are determined similarly, but also affected by the preferences. Before the release of the complete simulator, we will incorporate differential privacy throughout the pipeline.

---

[2] https://dbh.hkdir.no/dbh-old/dokumentasjon/tabell.action?tabellId=379.

[3] Note that about 30% of the applications are of local admission, which means that the acceptance offers are made by each institution individually and not as part of the centralised process. Local admission is performed for master's programs or for special programs in which admission is based on additional criteria such as interviews.

[4] https://dbh.hkdir.no/dbh-old/dokumentasjon/tabell.action?tabellId=472.

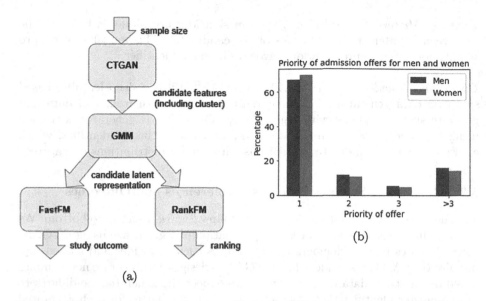

Fig. 1. (a) Simulator pipeline diagram. (b) A possible analysis to perform on the simulated data. The priority of admission offers made according to gender, using original data with 0.01-differential privacy using the Laplace mechanism.

3.1 Prepossessing and Training

We provide details of how the selected models are trained from the bottom up:

RankFM. We train rankFM[5], a factorisation machine model designed for ranked data with a loss function based on pairwise comparisons [10], to predict candidates' preferences over study programs. This model considers implicit data: a pairwise comparison is performed between programs ranked by the candidate and programs not ranked by that candidate, such that the latter are considered to have a lower priority. The comparison between ranked programs is not performed explicitly and is only addressed by giving larger confidence weights to higher ranked programs. Notably, rankFM allows us to incorporate candidates' features and study programs' features, such that their relation to candidates' preferences over programs is not lost. This model provides latent representations for candidates and study programs that, when combined, give a preference value for every student and university program pair.

FastFM. We train fastFM [3], a factorisation machine model with root-mean-square error for explicit feedback, to predict the students' study outcomes. Here, the candidates' features and the study programs' features include the latent representation obtained from rankFM. The features also include the preferences. The outcomes may be defined as average first year grade, normalised in $[0, 1]$. New latent representations of candidates and programs are provided by fastFM.

---

[5] https://github.com/etlundquist/rankfm.

Gaussian Mixture Model (GMM). A Gaussian Mixture Model is fitted to the concatenated latent representations of the candidates. This model allows us to sample new latent representations given a Gaussian identifier.

Conditional Tabular GAN (CTGAN). CTGAN[6] [12] is a deep learning based synthetic data generator for tabular data, that can learn from real data and generate synthetic clones with high fidelity. The CTGAN generator is trained using the candidates' feature data, including a GMM cluster identifier, which allows to generate candidate populations with similar distributions of features.

3.2   Generating Student Features, Preferences and Outcomes

To generate a new population, we can now follow Fig. 1a from top to bottom. We generate individual features for a new population of a given size using CTGAN. These features include demographic attributes such as gender and citizenship, but also the GMM cluster identifier. CTGAN is designed to generate new samples based on the train data distribution, so we expect the generated candidates to have a cluster identifier that fits their other features. Then, for each generated candidate we sample the specific pretrained Gaussian according to the their GMM cluster identifiers. As a result, we get the latent representations which holds information regarding the preferences and outcomes of candidates. Using the precalculated latent representations for study programs, we can predict the ranking and outcome of the study programs for each generated candidate.

3.3   Simulating Admission Decisions (Work in Progress)

Given the preferences of candidates and study programs, we can run the Gale-Shapley matching algorithm, a variation of Stable Marriage Matching for the hospitals-residents problem [8], to simulate the current admission system in Norway. The output will simulate the offers made in the first admission round. Given an initial offer, the candidate may decide to decline the offer. To simulate the second phase of acceptance, we simulate offers to applicants for programs in order of the programs' preferences (point scheme). We will use a classifier to predict offer acceptance by students for both first and second phase study offers.

Note that for this simulation the programs point schemes as well as their capacity has to be known. Neither are provided in the data, but can be deduced by the properties of the procedure of admissions in Norway. If a candidate has been accepted by a program (independent of whether they accept the offer and in which phase the offer was made), then

1. any other qualified applicant that was not given a study offer must have a worse point score for the program, and
2. if there exist such an applicant as in (a), then the capacity of the program is equal to the number of students that accepted the study offer.

---

[6] https://github.com/sdv-dev/CTGAN.

By these observations, we gain pairwise comparisons between (qualified) candidates point scores for the different programs. We can then find program point schemes that are linear functions or polynomials over the candidate features that satisfy these relations. The capacities are either determined by (b) or can simply be assumed to be the number of students that accepted the study offer.

4   Fair Matchings

The simulator, if implemented as described in Sect. 3, can be used to generate realistic instances of hospital/residents or school choice problems on which algorithmic solutions can be tested.

Fairness is particularly relevant to centralised school choice mechanisms and can be analysed for different solutions. We do not propose here a specific measure of fairness, but rather facilitate the analysis of different fairness notions. Apart from the usual notion of stability which only relies on preferences of candidates and programs, one can consider more elaborate objectives, such as equal preference satisfaction across groups based on gender or other demographic attributes. For example, Fig. 1b shows the satisfaction difference between men and women for the current admission system (real data). We can see that the percent of women who are offered admission to their first priority is higher than the equivalent percent of men. Yet, it is reversed for lower priorities. A possible explanation would be that women place 'safer' choices as their top priorities. Additional analysis could include satisfaction differences among counties or age groups, admission differences and outcome differences.

Furthermore, the possibility to predict study outcomes opens up the possibility to find allocations that offer equal predicted study success across groups. As the point scoring system of university programs is intended to rank the candidates by their capability of studying, it would be interesting to consider how much the point scheme correlates with the predicted study success of the students. One can measure how different a matching based on predicted study success instead of point schemes for university program preferences would be.

5   Conclusion

The simulator presented here is planned to use a combination of factorisation machines and Gaussian mixture models to provide a real-world-based benchmark in a countrywide scale. Using this simulated data, one could measure welfare and fairness not only with respect to students' and university's preferences, but also with respect to their outcomes. We believe this simulator has the potential to advance the research efforts in school choice and illuminate new interesting problems that exist in current school assignment systems.

Acknowledgements. This work was supported by the Research Council of Norway under project number 302203. We are thankful for the data provided by the Norwegian Directorate for Higher Education and Skills.

References

1. Homepage: Database for statistics on higher education (database for statistikk om høyere utdanning). https://dbh.hkdir.no/. Accessed 01 May 2022
2. Homepage: Norwegian universities and colleges admission service. https://www.samordnaopptak.no/info/english/. Accessed 27 Apr 2022
3. Bayer, I.: fastFM: a library for factorization machines. J. Mach. Learn. Res. **17**(1), 6393–6397 (2016)
4. Biró, P., et al.: First handbook of the cost action CA15210: European network for collaboration on kidney exchange programmes (ENCKEP). European Cooperation in Science and Technology, Brussels (2017)
5. Biró, P.: University admission practices – Hungary, MiP country profile 5 (2011). https://www.matching-in-practice.eu/higher-education-in-hungary/. Accessed 28 Apr 2022
6. Gale, D., Shapley, L.S.: College admissions and the stability of marriage. Am. Math. Monthly **69**(1), 9–15 (1962). http://www.jstor.org/stable/2312726
7. Larroucau, T., Rios, I.: Dynamic college admissions and the determinants of students' college retention. Technical report 2020 and, Do "Short-List" Students Report Truthfully (2020)
8. Manlove, D.: Algorithmics of Matching Under Preferences. Series on theoretical computer science. World Scientific (2013). https://books.google.no/books?id=7wGJMAEACAAJ
9. Samordna opptak: Wikipedia article: Norwegian universities and colleges admission service. https://en.wikipedia.org/wiki/Norwegian_Universities_and_Colleges_Admission_Service. Accessed 27 Apr 2022
10. Rendle, S., Freudenthaler, C.: Improving pairwise learning for item recommendation from implicit feedback. In: Proceedings of the 7th ACM International Conference on Web Search and Data Mining, pp. 273–282 (2014)
11. Terrier, C.: Matching practices for secondary public school teachers – France, MiP country profile 20 (2014). https://www.matching-in-practice.eu/matching-practices-of-teachers-to-schools-france/. Accessed 28 Apr 2022
12. Xu, L., Skoularidou, M., Cuesta-Infante, A., Veeramachaneni, K.: Modeling tabular data using conditional GAN. In: Advances in Neural Information Processing Systems, vol. 32 (2019)

Author Index